STORY MASTERY

STORY MASTERY

How leaders supercharge results
with business storytelling

Yamini Naidu

Published by Yamini Naidu Consulting
support@yamininaidu.com.au
www.yamininaidu.com.au

9780648598701 (paperback)
9780648598718 (ebook)

A catalogue record for this
book is available from the
National Library of Australia

Cover, text design and typesetting by Jen Clark Design
Edited by Jem Bates

For my brother Prathap Sunder and my sister Girija Bhaskar
whose humour, generosity and stories light me up

CONTENTS

ABOUT THE AUTHOR

Yamini Naidu is the world's only economist turned business story-teller and is rated among the top three business storytellers globally.

With a client list of Fortune 500 and ASX Top-100 companies, she works at board and CEO level around the world, moving leaders from spreadsheets to stories.

Her previous books, *Power Play: Game changing influence strategies for leaders* and the bestseller *Hooked: How leaders connect, engage & inspire using storytelling*, were published internationally by John Wiley & Sons.

A global citizen, Yamini was born and raised in Mumbai (formerly Bombay) in India and is a gold medalist from University of Bombay and both a scholarship winner and a postgraduate from the London School of Economics.

She has lived, worked, studied and travelled in India, Asia, Europe and the Americas. She now lives in Melbourne, Australia, with her large extended family and a crazy cavoodle named Ace. Yamini is also a voluntary guide at the National Gallery of Victoria (NGV).

When she travels for work she misses her family, her dog and Melbourne's famous coffee.

ACKNOWLEDGEMENTS

Blue azure seas, the boat glides to a stop. We disembark. Waiting staff line the pathway. They hold trays of chilled drinks and greet us with big smiles: 'Welcome to Nurai island.'

In Arabic, *nur* means light. I pinch myself. Am I presenting in Paradise? The training room is outdoors, set under the shade of a beautiful canopy. Artfully scattered banana lounges, deep cushions and low-slung chaise longues provide the seating. There's a deep wooden bar running along one end. Behind me, an infinity pool, metres from the beach and the inviting blue of the Arabian Sea. I joke with the participants, 'The only thing standing between the beer, the beach and the bar is me!'

In this breathtaking setting, they are all riveted. Not by me (I'm not that immodest!), but by each other's stories. 'It's not a workshop – it's a fun shop!' declares one participant.

This storytelling session is for Macquarie Telecom Group's high achievers, who are recognised and rewarded for their contribution to the company's success (Macquarie Club). It is also an opportunity for these high achievers to spend time learning from and with each other in an amazing overseas setting. And that's why I'm there, in the sun and sand, doing the thing that lights them and me up – sharing stories.

I am privileged to work with leaders like these all over the world, from my hometown of Melbourne to Ford HQ in Michigan and everywhere in between. A big thank you to all my clients who engage me daily to work with them and their teams.

A deep thank you to my clients who have so generously allowed me to share their stories in this book. I also want to acknowledge and honour Noeleen Carey, Lisa Leong and John Sands who believe in the power of storytelling and gave me the privilege and pleasure of working with their organisations.

I humbly acknowledge the greats in storytelling who have guided and shaped my work: Steve Denning (who pioneered the field), and thank you Annette Simpson for your wisdom and generosity.

To my wisdom council, whose advice and encouragement I lean on – Carolyn Tate, Kath Walters and Sandy McDonald. To my friends especially the Awesome Foursome and the GIF Girls (Anna, Kim and Linda), thank you for putting up with my early-morning texts and random GIFS – your love and laughter keep me sane.

But most of all to my family, whose love and support ground me. Every time I return from a trip – whether criss-crossing the globe or just the Melbourne CBD – I unlock the front door and am greeted by a crazy dog and my family demanding 'What's for a dinner?' It's an in-joke yet it makes my heart sing, because I know I'm home and I'm loved.

Finally, thank you, dear reader, for choosing this book and for taking that first step towards Story Mastery.

INTRODUCTION

How do we persuade people to adopt our ideas, listen to what we have to say and be inspired into action?

To answer, I want to take you back in time. To May 27, 1992. Vedran Smailovic was in his upstairs apartment in downtown Sarajevo. Without warning, a mortar round exploded in the street outside. Vedran, shaken by the blast, ran to his window and looked out through the smoke onto a scene of horror. Twenty-two people – friends and neighbours, who moments before had been standing in a queue to buy bread – lay dead.

It was a time of war, and Sarajevo had become ground zero in the conflict. For Vedran, the terror of war had finally struck home. He felt helpless and fearful. But then he decided to act. He would do what he knew how to do – make music. Vedran was principal cellist for the Sarajevo Opera.

The next day, dressed in formal attire as if for a concert performance, he stepped out of his apartment block, cello in one hand and a small plastic stool in the other. Vedran crossed the street to the bomb site opposite his apartment. There, in full public view, amidst the shelling and sniper fire of war-ravaged Sarajevo, Vedran Smailovic sat down and started to play.

He would play for 22 consecutive days, to honour each victim of the bakery bombing. As he played, after a few days, the city ground to a standstill. The snipers held off; the bombing stopped and the madness of war gave way briefly to the magic of music. Slowly, in ones and twos, other musicians joined him. Soon almost every member of the Sarajevo Opera orchestra who was still alive was playing with him.

Vedran playing his cello in the rubble painted a vivid picture in my mind. When I heard his story, it drew goosebumps and tears.

Vedran Smailovic ... a leader of exceptional bravery making a difference in a dangerous world. His story teaches us that as leaders we should be prepared to do something very different for success. We have a mandate to change our world through our work. Just as he did.

Most of us are lucky enough not to live in a war zone, where lives are daily in the balance. Yet our work matters, to us, our teams and our organisations. As smart professionals we always want to know:

- What is it we are *not* doing that we should do?
- What are we currently doing that sabotages our success?

These questions may sound contradictory, yet success nests in the crosshairs of the tension between them. Why do you need to do something different? As for Vedran, it probably sounds dangerous, foolhardy even.

John Cage famously said, 'I can't understand why people are frightened of new ideas. I'm frightened of the old ones'. There is grave danger in maintaining the status quo. These are the three traps awaiting leaders who persist in doing what they have always done.

THREE TRAPS

Let's look at the three traps and the solution to eliminating all three.

Keeping tigers away

In *The Cheeky Monkey: Writing Narrative Comedy*, author Tim Ferguson shares this anecdote: 'A man sits on the train throwing biscuits out of the window. A woman asks, "Why are you doing that?" "To keep the tigers away," he replies. The woman frowns and says, "There are no tigers in Australia." "See, it's working!" the man responds.'

Sometimes the tasks we do at work are unnecessary. We may do them out of habit, or fear. The tasks don't give us results. Not only are they unnecessary, but they're also a colossal waste of time, effort and resources. Yet they have a hold on us – they are our metaphorical tigers.

Sisyphus' slippery slope

In Greek mythology, Sisyphus was the king of Ephyra whom the gods punished for his deceitfulness. His punishment was to push a boulder up a great hill. As he neared the top he would lose control of it and it would roll back down, and he would have to start again … and so on, for eternity. This too-familiar scenario is every leader's nightmare – having all your efforts come to naught. Not just once but repeatedly, endlessly.

Albert Einstein defined insanity as 'doing the same thing over and over again and expecting different results'. The only way we can regain our agency is to try something we haven't thought of or even considered before.

The drunkard's search

A police officer sees a drunken man intently searching the ground near a lamppost and asks him what he is looking for. The man replies that he is looking for his car keys, and the officer helps for a few minutes without success. Then the police officer asks the man whether he is certain he dropped the keys near the lamppost. 'No,' comes the reply, 'I lost the keys somewhere across the street'. 'Why look here then?' asks the surprised and irritated officer. 'The light is much better here,' the intoxicated man responds, as if stating the obvious.

Abraham Kaplan, the first philosopher to examine behavioural sciences systematically, referred to this as 'the principle of the drunkard's search', a type of observational bias that occurs when people search for something only where it is easiest to look.

Recognising these three traps challenges us to:

- stop wasting time on the unnecessary (keeping tigers away)
- stop expecting different results from the same strategies (Sisyphus' slippery slope)
- stop looking for answers in the most obvious or easy places (the drunkard's search).

Why bother? No matter what you do at work, it is always about engaging people and delivering results. Success is about relationships and results.

Business storytelling helps us to stop wasting time on the unnecessary (more PowerPoint-heavy presentation stacks, overloading our audiences with ever-more information). Storytelling gives us a different strategy that is fresh and relatable in business, so we are not condemned to Sisyphus' fate, putting in the hard yards and wondering why it's not working. And storytelling helps us avoid the drunkard's search: it is not the most obvious or easiest place to look, but it will give us the richest rewards.

Storytelling is for you if:

- You never want to hear the words 'I still don't get this' again.
- You want to connect, engage and inspire people.
- You want to move people to action.
- You want people to be on board – to invest emotionally.
- You want to translate data so it's compelling.
- You want people awake and listening, not dozing through your next presentation.
- You want people to understand and embrace the strategy.
- You want to touch people's hearts.
- You crave personal and professional impact.
- You want to create a legacy through your work.

Storytelling is NOT for you if:

- You want to manipulate people.
- You want to use it for evil, not good.
- You have a 'God complex'!

HMM, STORYTELLING?

The word storytelling conjures up many images and has many associations, both positive and negative. Let me clarify right here and now that the storytelling we are talking about in this book is Business Storytelling. Storytelling with a purpose and for results. This is definitely not once-upon-a-time fairy stories, fantasies or war stories about the good old times at work. If you are doing any of these in the work context, cease and desist immediately.

Stephen Denning laid the foundations for the field of business storytelling in 2005 with his book *The Leader's Guide to Storytelling*. Business storytelling is the practical application of appropriate, purposeful (on message) short stories in the work context. The stories support your data; they don't take the place of data but add to it. Phew! I can hear your sigh of relief.

Here is a story shared by one of my clients.

STORY TITLE: STEP BACK AND PAUSE

My little five-year-old niece Maya walked into the house yesterday, holding a ripe apple in each hand. I thought this would be the perfect time to role model sharing! I asked her, 'Maya, can I please have an apple?' She looked at me and immediately bit into the apple in her right hand. Then just as quickly she took a bite out of the apple in her left hand. I was shocked. But before I could react she held out the apple in her left hand, saying, 'Here aunty, take this one – it's sweeter'.
I'm sharing this because so often we jump to conclusions about people's behaviour. Imagine if sometimes we took a step back and paused. The difference that could make.

STORYTELLER: B. ISKANDER

This is a great example of a business story. Iskander was thinking about how to give her team a different way of approaching their work.

While it paid to be efficient with their decision making, sometimes they needed to step back, look again and perhaps re-evaluate things. Pass on that advice, and it is Teflon – it simply won't stick. People will agree with the idea, then immediately forget it. It will wash over them and away with all the other instruction and communication debris that floods their day.

The human brain, this amazing, discerning, sense-making machine, ignores all the 'blah, blah'. A good story, on the other hand, is pure velcro. When you share a story, people connect with it in the moment. With a good story, your audience's attention is palpable. They listen with their hearts. They think about what you have said – and it sparks an 'aha' in their hearts and minds. What's more, they remember it and will often retell it.

In chaos theory, the butterfly effect refers to the way a small change in one state (a butterfly beats its wings) can produce a very large effect (a tsunami) in a later one. In communication, business storytelling is the butterfly effect. That is what a story can do for you.

Sadly, the main theme of the feedback I get from leaders all over the world is regret. They wish they had discovered storytelling earlier in their career. All this time, like Sisyphus, they have been pushing their boulder uphill only to see their efforts come to naught.

So if you are ready to take a quantum leap in your impact and influence, if you're hungry to try something different, even revolutionary, to supercharge your results by learning business storytelling, then this book is for you.

WHAT MAKES ME AN EXPERT?

I am an economist by training (please don't stop reading here). As a senior leader in corporate Australia, I always felt frustrated that data alone didn't persuade people to change. The numbers made sense, the logical case for the new strategy was undeniable, then we'd hit our biggest stumbling block – people.

Yet that same stumbling block, people, is also the key to success. Whether it was persuading people to clean up after themselves in the tearoom, or to embrace the new vision for 2020, we always hit the same hurdle. Leadership would be dead easy if we could tell people what to do and they did it! But that's never the case, is it?

Something needed to change. All my leadership peers shared my frustration. Leadership is about getting results through people. Inspiring them to act. Yet this was very hard to do. And even harder to do consistently well and with integrity. We were not a small pocket of outliers. This was not an anomaly. It was a universal frustration. Every organisation I have worked in faced this challenge, and the literature and research backed it up. It's what makes leadership hard, complex and challenging.

One day, before a long-haul flight, I made an impulse purchase at the airport bookstore: it was Stephen Denning's *The Leader's Guide to Storytelling*. The title intrigued me. I scoffed at the audacity of the idea of storytelling in business – my economist's brain recoiled – but I was also desperate for answers. So desperate I would look at anything, even if it sounded like snake oil.

I read – no, *devoured* – the book on that flight. This is not normal for me, as I routinely alternate between work, play and sleep on my business travels. And as I was reading the book a light bulb exploded in my head. Could storytelling be the missing link? As soon as I disembarked I began to ring leaders I knew, in what became a series of chaotic, overexcited and barely coherent calls. I wanted to talk about and share this idea. Storytelling in business – what did they think? (You know who you are, and thanks again for your insight, your generosity and your patience.)

Every leader I spoke to that day and in the following weeks (yes, I had become obsessed) said the same thing: 'We all know good leaders tell stories, but *we* don't know how to'. This personal discovery for me coincided with Barack Obama's election as US President. A revolutionary moment in American and world politics, it also saw the recognition of storytelling as a credible force for change, with commentator after commentator noting Obama's skills as a storyteller.

I was desperate to learn about this force. Not any old tale-telling but *business storytelling – storytelling with a purpose and for results*. There was absolutely no one offering it in the Australian market. There was evidently a niche, and I saw no one filling it. What better way to learn something than to teach it? So on that brave premise, I co-founded Australia's first storytelling company. Within 30 days of launching, Phil Davis of National Australia Bank engaged our services. A brilliant people leader who was in the vanguard of leadership practice, Davis was aware of this embryonic field of storytelling, and decided that this was just what he and his leadership team needed.

From that first humble workshop, with every client I grew, learned and shared their successes. The three things I have learned that make this book critical for your personal and professional success:

- Using stories (short, compelling, authentic and purposeful stories) along with numbers or data will help you quantum leap your professional success.
- Storytelling is a skill you can learn and teach, and we can all get better at it.
- Storytelling gives you exponential results.

I have seen this again and again with my clients in organisations from Fortune 500 companies to start-ups, with leaders all over the world, in different countries and contexts. I've seen it when they won the pitch against all odds or induced previously reticent investors to empty their wallets or even persuaded a reluctant 10-year-old to make his bed in the morning! Their reaction is universal and predictable: 'I have tried *everything*. I can't believe how when I told a story it worked.'

Storytelling expert Annette Simmons calls it 'magic maths': using stories, 1 minute plus 1 minute does not equal 2 minutes of information; rather, it gives an exponential return on investment.

In economics, we are always seeking the sweet spot between effectiveness and effort. Nothing expresses this better than the Pareto principle, which states that 20 per cent of your efforts will yield 80 per cent of your results. As a leader and a business professional, the one tool that will reliably give you that 80 per cent lift is storytelling.

In this book I channel a decade of experience, insights, practical skills and techniques. Having collaborated with leaders all over the world, I know what works, and importantly what doesn't work, with business storytelling. Business storytelling is a skill, and if there is only one new skill you decide to master in business, make it this one.

WHAT AND WHY MASTERY?

Rebecca Rothstein is a private wealth advisor. *Forbes* named her one of 'America's Top Wealth Advisors' in 2017 and the '#1 Top Women's Wealth Advisor' in 2018. For Rothstein, 'Mastery is patience, perseverance and leaving your ego at the door'.

I believe in the idea that when you do something, you do it well. You do it to the best of your ability. Being a story master will help you stand out in a crowded marketplace. It will elevate your leadership and professional reputation and results. Why settle for less than mastery? You can be bad at storytelling, or mediocre, but I'm not interested in that part of the bell curve. If you want to be at the peak performance mastery point on the curve, then keep reading!

Yes, it will still take patience and perseverance, but this book will show you how to fast-track your mastery, to take the hard out of hard work, so what would take you 10,000 hours on your own, learning painfully from your mistakes and setbacks, can be achieved in a fraction of the time.

While I speed up your mastery I also invite you to leave your ego at the door. Great storytellers operate from humility and being true to themselves. It might sound new-agey, but after a decade working at the coal face of senior leadership, I know this is true.

PREPARE FOR THE REVOLUTION

Today you can't throw a stone without hitting a storytelling consultant, yet I remember a lot of blank stares when I co-founded Australia's first storytelling company 10 years ago. The first 18 months were spent answering puzzled questions such as, 'How can you use stories in business?' and 'Aren't storytellers born, so you either have it or you don't?'

Today we know you can storytell in business, and you should if you want to connect with and inspire your audience. Storytelling is not a natural gift, but everyone can learn how to do it better. Even those who appear natural and spontaneous are seasoned and practised in their craft. The preparation may have happened in a conscious, focused way in the background or have built up over a lifetime. We see only the end results, not the hard work that went into it, so we assume these people are 'naturally' talented.

It's wonderful to see how in just the past decade the role of business storytelling has become established in both business and leadership. It is now widely taught across the globe and has a place in most leadership development programs. This begs the question, what's next for business storytelling?

We are going to experience a tsunami of storytelling across all platforms, digital media and sectors, including marketing, advertising and professional services, to name a few. Stories will be as necessary as data. No one is going to buy or be persuaded to change simply based on data. Consumers and audiences are more curious, demanding and impatient than ever before. For business professionals, this means audiences are also tougher to reach and tougher to please.

'Show me the money' will be reinvented as 'Tell me the story'. Google's own ad on 'Search Stories' is a wonderful example of this. Instead of showcasing their technology, they tell a story of romance. Through a series of screenshots of Google searches, the ad tells the story of how a young American's plan to study in Paris leads to love and marriage, and a final search on how to assemble a baby's crib.

Storytelling is the fuel that drives compelling engagement both face to face and on social media. This means our audiences are going to be much more discerning. The authentic, well-told story will wow. Spin passed off as stories will incur well-deserved derision. Social media will amplify success and failure.

So where will storytelling be one year from now? Here's my snapshot:

- more competition (everyone will be doing it across industries, in roles from leadership to marketing)
- more discerning audiences, who will also be more vocal
- (this is the biggie) a chasm between good, bad and ugly storytelling.

How will you prepare for this storytelling revolution? This book is the best first step you can take.

HOW THIS BOOK WORKS

I want to make a confession at this point, believing it's always good to begin a relationship with a clean slate. The truth is, I have made some assumptions about you, dear reader:

- First, you are hungry. You want to learn what else you can do at work to build on your success.
- You are pragmatic. You want practical, step-by-step advice backed by solid research.
- You want to hear of real examples from leaders like you – where they used stories, what the stories were and why they worked.
- You are not scared of the dark stuff. You also want to learn when not to use stories and why some stories don't work.
- You want to learn, but it's got to be fun and easy, with a dash of sass (I'm big on sass).
- You are big enough for tough love. You want someone to be straight with you and not sugar-coat stuff. I only do tough love.
- You are smart enough to take this, do the work and apply it in your context.

Ticking these boxes? A warm welcome to you!

Unsexy advice

I recently had the pleasure of getting some advice on building a career in comedy (I know!) from Dave O'Neil. We were asking about what appeared to be the overnight success of some comedians. He said, 'The secret really boils down to three things: work hard, be consistent and be nice to people.'

I realised this is true of every venture in life. I loved how he said you have to be ready to work hard. Sounds as old fashioned as your grandma's doilies? Doing the work is not as seductive as shortcut get-rich schemes and life hacks that guarantee to transform all our frogs into princes. No one ever plugs a get-rich-slow scheme, because that smacks of work. In fact, often the systems, books and advice make it sound like *no* work is involved. No one actually mentions *doing the work!*

So I'm going to be deeply unsexy in my advice. What matters is doing the work. On the secret of his success, Michael Jordan said simply, 'I put the ball in the hole,' which is another way of saying 'I do the work'.

Doing the work is rarely raised explicitly. Either that is assumed or they are selling us snake oil. But work is first, foremost and always. Of course, it has to be purposeful work you love and are passionate about – but most of all it is work.

For writers, that means spending hours writing every day, even when you don't feel like it. For speakers, it means earning your speaking stripes for years on all sorts of gigs (hello, Rotary and Probus clubs). In comedy, it means hitting open mic nights every week, no matter where you are in the world. Even when you'd rather cocoon yourself in your hotel room binge-watching Netflix with a glass of red and ordering room service! (Not bitter, only observing.)

I don't want to give the impression that doing the work is grim, gruelling and thankless. By doing the work, we experience all the beautiful things life has to offer through discovery, learning and growth. We face the demons of procrastination and self-doubt, and transcend them to make a contribution.

In this book, though, I will make the work easy, exciting – and possible. For this book (or any other book/system/advice) to work, you have to be willing to do the work. This is the only commitment you need to make for results, success and mastery. Muhammad Ali said, 'The fight is won or lost far away from witnesses – behind the lines, in the gym, and out there on the road, long before I dance under those lights.'

We are at the crossroads now. If you are ready to do the work with me, I promise you a great ride. We will learn, laugh and taste success every inch of the way. I promise you we won't be limping but taking a running jump into story success. I'll hold your hand and make this journey easy and possible. I'll even guarantee success.

Caution, people at work

Like all authors, I want you to read and savour every word, apply my advice and reap the rewards. But I am also a realist! This book is organised in a linear way, so it will be most useful if you read the chapters in the order I present them, especially if you are new to storytelling. If you have worked with me or are familiar with storytelling principles, you can scan the first three chapters, then dig deep from chapter 4 onwards, where stories are deconstructed. The final chapter (*Mastery to artistry*) is for overachievers who want to move beyond mastery. But don't start there! It would be like trying to leap to the top of a ladder without using the intervening steps. Chapters 1 through 11 cover the why, what and how of storytelling. You may find more than you need to be a story master there. Then you can move on to chapter 12.

I have made this book as easy to navigate as possible, because I know you are time poor, want quick results and are juggling complex priorities. There is plenty of help on hand to find your way smoothly to the destination marked 'Story Master'.

Hashtag help

Watch out for the hashtag #StoryMastery. This is to prompt you to stop and think and be conscious of the point I'm making. It's my way of highlighting something important. Think of it as a worker in a high-visibility vest with a STOP sign. Always do a double take and re-read anything with this hashtag.

Forgetting and remembering

There is a craft and an art to storytelling, and to master it merits a whole book (this book, in fact). I also want you to know that help is at hand, but from an unexpected source, because this time it's not me – it's you.

In her book *Drawing on the Right Side of the Brain*, Betty Edwards shares this charming anecdote from arts teacher Howard Ikemoto: 'When my daughter was about seven years old, she asked me one day what I did at work. I told her I worked at the college, that my job was to teach people how to draw. She stared back at me, incredulous, and said, "You mean they forgot?"'

The same thing happens to us at work. We storytell in the pub, or with friends and family, but when we are at work we forget this innate ability. While not all our stories are directly transportable to work (yes, I am saying no to that risqué, non-PC story), at some level we already intuitively know the fundamentals of the business story. So this is about rediscovery as well as learning new concepts and ideas. These two journeys, unlocking what we know and learning new skills, will help us become story masters.

Playing with all the ladders

Storytelling is like playing snakes and ladders and getting all the ladders. Not using storytelling is like playing snakes and ladders with lots of snakes and not a ladder in sight. I'll give you all the ladders you need. Let's get shaking our story tail feathers to success!

Key insights

Every chapter finishes by summarising its key insights and ideas as a revision aid. It's a quick checklist capturing the main ideas in each chapter.

Reach out

I'm literally an email away from you. So please reach out via LinkedIn or email. Let me know how you're going and if you have any questions. I love hearing from my readers and celebrating your successes.

1. WHY STORYTELLING?

Research has found that leaders around the world consistently identify very similar challenges, even though they describe them differently. Heading the list are usually:

- leading a team
- guiding change
- inspiring others.

Is it all about engaging and connecting people? Yes. It's about relationships *and* results.

If you were a leader in 16th century Italy, the answer to moving people into action was easy. You would do it through fear, as suggested by diplomat and political theorist, Niccolo Machiavelli. Successful, smart leaders in the 21st century know that hard power (fear, command and control, yell and tell) is not the way to create long-lasting, sustainable influence or change.

In the 1990s, political scientist Joseph Nye introduced us to the concept of soft power – creating change through connecting, consulting and collaborating. Most leaders know this is how we get people on board. Think of soft power as sowing seeds when planting a garden: it's difficult for the impatient but worth it for the long-term results.

Yet research tells us that more than 70 per cent of change efforts in organisations fail. So whatever combination of these two tools (hard power and soft power) we adopt, many of our efforts will still be unsuccessful. Hard and soft power alone are often not enough.

The new currency of change is as old as time. It is storytelling. A purposeful, authentic story in business can influence, persuade and motivate people. Here's an example from a client on what this looks like.

STORY TITLE: CRASH AND CURTSY

When I was 22, I became a travelling saleswoman. I'd won a big promotion to work in Australia. After spending the previous few weeks selling in Utah, you can imagine my desire for a fancy international business trip. Bright eyed and bushy tailed, I landed in gorgeous sunny Sydney.

I started at the University of New South Wales and pitched to class after class, slowly working my way up to the larger lecture halls. Finally, I was ready to hit the biggest 1000-seat hall on campus. I was so excited. I ran into the room, up the ramp, jumped across to the stage and BOOM! I promptly missed the stage and landed flat on my bum. Turns out there was a gap I'd missed. A thousand soon-to-be engineers burst out laughing. Now I had a choice to make: run, freeze or keep going. I climbed up onto that stage, curtsied to all (everyone clapped) and began my pitch. You may wonder why I've shared this story with you today? AMP Capital is changing, rapidly. And not all of those changes will land perfectly. But it's the power to pick ourselves up, to keep going, that's what matters.

STORYTELLER: MICHELLE SANIT, CHANGE MANAGER,
STRATEGY & INVESTMENT SERVICES, AMP CAPITAL

John Kotter, the foremost authority on change leadership, suggests change leaders communicate 'in ways that are as emotionally engaging and compelling as possible. They rely on vivid stories that are told and retold. You don't have to spend a million dollars and six months to prepare for a change effort. You do have to make sure that you touch people emotionally ... '

> Hard power informs, soft power invites and story power inspires #StoryMastery

Not for a moment am I suggesting that in sharing one story you will influence 100 per cent of your audience. No one story can do that, and no one deserves that level of influence, because one day you might have a bad idea. But time and again when working with clients I have seen how purposeful stories, crafted and shared with authenticity, inspire and have a seismic impact.

The currency of business itself has changed. Are you trading in this new currency?

WHY TODAY?

For nearly 80 years, the Harvard Study of Adult Development has been collecting data on the physical and mental health of hundreds of men and women and drawing lessons on how we might live longer and happier lives. Three words capture the findings: relationships, relationships, relationships!

This insight is the key to our success at work. No matter what you do, your success depends on your relationships (how you connect, engage and inspire people) and the results you deliver. This is what you are measured by, what gets you promoted and noticed. And the two are directly correlated, as my statistician lecturer was fond of shouting out at us:

Relationships + Results = Success

Engaging people and delivering results. Day in, day out. We engage our teams, our peers, our boards, our suppliers, our customers, our stakeholders, our communities. We cannot get the results we need without relationships.

Psychologist professor Robert Hogan identifies our primary concerns at work as *getting along* and *getting ahead*. 'We want to get along with others by getting a good reputation and then we want to get ahead using that reputation.' Again, relationships (getting along) and results (getting ahead).

So how can storytelling help us build relationships and deliver results? As leaders we know our results happen through other people – we drive them, motivate them, inspire them, give them direction, collaborate, consult … the list goes on.

Where does storytelling fit into this heady mix? The words of Antoine de Saint-Exupéry come to mind: 'If you want to build a ship,' he wrote, 'don't drum up people to collect wood and don't assign them tasks and work, but rather teach them to long for the endless immensity of the sea.' We have seen this time and time again: in JFK's 'man on the moon' moment, Martin Luther King's 'I have a dream' speech, Barack Obama's (and Bob the Builder's) 'Yes We Can' slogan. All such appeals have made us yearn for the sea.

How are you going with making people yearn for the sea? The following model from Aristotle helps us understand where we are failing. I'm not so vain as to assume you have read my previous best-selling (so glad I could weave that in) book *Hooked: How leaders connect, engage and inspire using storytelling*. Those of you who have may remember this model from there, but it is so important to our practice as leaders and professionals that it bears revisiting.

ARISTOTLE'S THREE MODES OF PERSUASION

Aristotle said you need three elements to influence or persuade, to make an impact:

- *logos* – logical reasoning
- *ethos* – personal credibility
- *pathos* – emotional connection.

Logos in business is the data, the facts and figures, the cost–benefit analysis – everything that sings to my economist's heart! It appeals to our logical, linear left brain too. In business, *logos* is critical and we do it well. We always lead with data, PowerPoint, information, charts (who doesn't love a good pie chart?), features and benefits, research – and more data.

Ethos is personal credibility. Read those words again. Not positional but personal. Positional credibility is your job title. But how believable are you? Do people trust you? Do you know (or sound like you know) what you are talking about? That's your personal credibility.

> Positional credibility opens doors, but personal credibility seals the deal #StoryMastery

Pathos is about creating an emotional connection. It means appealing to an audience's emotions. When Apple CEO Tim Cook described *sitting* as 'the new cancer', he loaded the relatively innocuous act with negative emotion – the fear raised by the spectre of cancer.

FIGURE 1.1: ARISTOTLE'S MODEL OF INFLUENCE

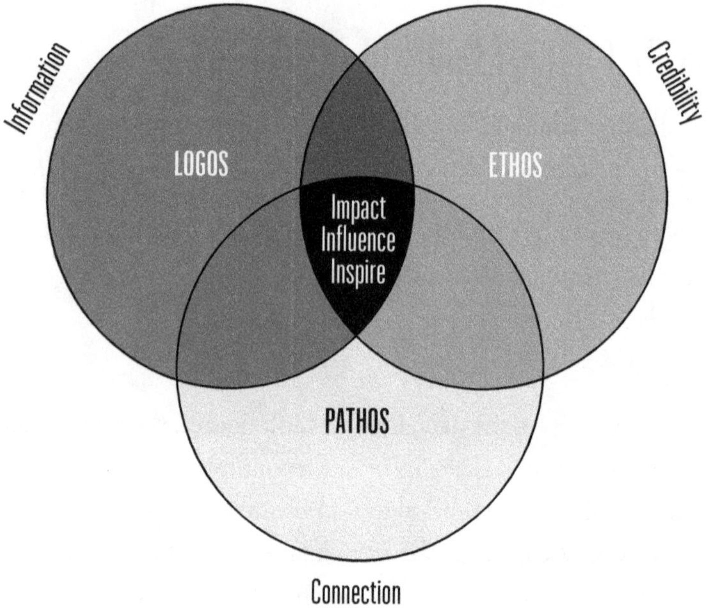

Connection

Consider all the ways you communicate, persuade and influence, inside and outside your organisation. In which of these three buckets – *logos*, *ethos* and *pathos* – do you and your organisation invest most of your time, money and effort? If you are like most leaders and organisations all over the world, you'll be putting a giant tick in the *logos* bucket.

Two and half thousand years ago Aristotle proposed that *logos* was *numero uno* in influencing people. But this is no cause for self-congratulation – unless you and your workplace have time travelled back to ancient Greece.

In today's context, *ethos* – personal credibility – plays the most important role. Trust me before you trust my message. And *ethos* beats *pathos* by a hair's breadth. Please, we need *logos*, *ethos* and *pathos* in business, but currently we are sitting on a one-legged stool called *logos*. And we get frustrated when our best efforts are failing. When the *logos* doesn't work, what do we do? We do more *logos*. Drowning your audience in data hasn't worked to persuade them, so let's amp up the volume. More of the same. More of what's not working. When has that ever worked?

It is important to understand how these three elements differ, and why *logos* just on its own isn't enough. *Logos* informs people, but it doesn't shift behaviour. If it did, no one would smoke (yet people do) or drive above the speed limit (yes, we have all been guilty), and we would all eat well and exercise every day (trying, but we are only human!). *Logos* on its own does not bring about change.

> To shift behaviour, we have to look at *ethos* and *pathos*
> #StoryMastery

But it's very hard for business people to 'do' *ethos* and *pathos*. You build up personal credibility (*ethos*) over time. People work with you, they find you deliver on your word, and that cements your credibility. Yet one misstep and that credibility can be destroyed overnight.

In a fast-paced, disrupted, time-poor business world, you rarely have the luxury of time. You might be a new leader in an organisation or have new people on your team. You might pitch to a room full of stakeholders, not all of whom know you, or you might meet a new client for the first time. In these contexts, the simplest yet most powerful way to fast-track *ethos* and create an emotional connection with your audience (*pathos*) is through a story.

I face this every day, wherever I am in the world, when I walk into a meeting cold. The people who engage me know my work, but the audience don't. They might have Googled and got the '*logos*' on me. In the first couple of minutes in front of an audience I have to establish *ethos* and create *pathos* around my message. I have learned to eat my own dog food. This is the story I sometimes open with.

STORY TITLE: 2 LETTERS, 10 WORDS

When I was 10, my teacher Miss Asha asked us to write a sentence that made sense, but the sentence could contain only 10 words, and each word could have only two letters. We tried and we tried and came up with nothing. My teacher then wrote on the board, 'If it is to be, it is up to me'. That day Miss Asha influenced a classroom full of children to think and behave differently. Not just in that moment but for the rest of their lives. It was my first lesson in influence and leadership, and I was hooked!

STORYTELLER: YAMINI NAIDU

In sharing this story I'm showing that influence is something I believe in and not just a current bandwagon for me. It also creates *pathos* in the room. The audience thinks about when they have been influenced by other people – teachers, mentors – and how that learning has stayed with them.

I have found that every time I share the Aristotle model of influence, the energy in the room explodes. Leaders pound their foreheads. All at once they can see the glaring gap in their practice, where they are falling short and why. Relying on *logos* alone is like trying to start a car on an empty tank. So frustrating. *Logos* is not enough. To succeed we have to fast-track both *ethos* and *pathos*. Current research supports this classic model.

DO MORE OR DO DIFFERENT?

In *Great at Work: How Top Performers Work Less and Achieve More*, author Morten Hansen points to the limitations of *logos*. We use logic and data to persuade, Hansen says, but 'If they "don't get it" we hammer our argument even harder.' The mistake we make is using more of the same tools that didn't work the first time! More emails, PowerPoints, reports etc. He argues, 'Communicating more of the same when people are not listening or accepting our message doesn't seem like a smart way to work.'

In Hansen's study he found the best advocates – those he called 'forceful champions' – inspired people and garnered support by appealing to their emotions as well as their rational minds. His advice? Don't do more – do different. Don't work harder – work smarter. My advice? Work smarter with storytelling.

I could rest the case for storytelling right here, but as the man selling steak knives would say, *Wait, there's more!*

THE CURSE OF KNOWLEDGE

In the 1990s Elizabeth Newton conducted an experiment at Stanford University titled 'Tappers and listeners'. She enlisted 500 volunteers and organised them into 250 pairs of tappers and listeners. She gave the tappers a list of popular songs ('Happy birthday', 'Jingle bells' and so on), which they then had to tap out while the listener guessed the song. She asked the tappers how often they thought they would be successful, to which they replied 50 per cent of the time. It turned out that their success rate was 2.5 per cent.

Newton concludes the 'Tappers and listeners' exercise shows two things: first, we all overestimate our ability as communicators. Second, when we know something (in this case the title of the song) our knowledge curses us. We can't imagine what it's like *not* to know it.

The curse of knowledge is manifested across all our roles in life – from parent to child, from leader to team and from teacher to student. Given your level of skill, expertise and experience in your field, I have bad news for you: you are blighted by the curse of knowledge! We all are. When we know something – this might be our life's work – we are carrying a huge context piece in our heads that our audience doesn't have. So they cannot connect the dots as we do.

Revealing the curse of knowledge is an explosive moment in my workshops and masterclasses. It is a moment of raw honesty for us as leaders and business professionals to admit that, yes, we are infected by the curse of knowledge. It is the shadow side of our expertise.

I give leaders time to discuss examples of the curse of knowledge in their day-to-day work, where they have experienced it and where they might have unleashed it on others. Apologies to my IT friends, but IT is the first place that comes to people's minds. One of my clients shared a gem in this context. He was heading up a technical team and they put out an email to the entire organisation on a new process change. He got a one-line reply from the CEO that read, 'Please resend this in plain English'. Ouch! Harsh, but true.

This is not the time to point our fingers at others (IT is an easy scapegoat), but to reflect on our own work. How can we dodge the curse of knowledge? There are two ways. Learn nothing again and you should be fine. Just kidding.

The other way? Tell a story. Here's an example from one of my clients.

STORY TITLE: THE PRICE OF TOMATOES

It was a dreary winter's afternoon. I was 25 and living in London. I found myself in aisle four at my local Tesco supermarket, scanning the price of canned tomatoes: 20p for home brand, 30p for regular and 40p for organic. I reached into my pocket and rummaged around and found one 10p coin and a shiny Australian two-dollar coin. I sighed and wished I was back home in Australia. On the bottom shelf I spotted a bottle of passata that had been marked down to 10p. *10p!* I bought it and used it in a pasta sauce that night.

Now, many years later, when thinking about money – do I have enough? – I always think of that experience in London and know anything I have now is a privilege in comparison.

STORYTELLER: HONOR MARINO, CULTURE AND ENGAGEMENT SPECIALIST, TASMANIAN NETWORKS PTY LIMITED

BEYOND BINARY

Many of us work with people who want only the data, the facts. Sometimes leaders tell me, 'I'm ready, but I'm not sure my audience is.'

I'm asked by leaders all over the world, 'So do I stick with facts or tell stories?'

Most leaders stick with the data. This focus often stems from their subject or technical expertise, but it ensures little or no audience engagement and limited recall. A few leaders use stories only, and this can feel hollow – where is the data?

Data or stories? Heads or hearts? Much as we like to believe people are rational beings, and that appealing to their heads with logic should persuade them, we know this to be far from the truth. If logic alone did the trick, business life would be so much easier: we could tell people the logical thing to do and they would do it!

Sally Hogshead, the author of *How to Fascinate*, points to research suggesting that where 100 years ago our attention span was 20 minutes, today it is just nine seconds. Yes, you read that right: nine seconds. We have become mean, lean scanning machines – a survival mechanism that gets us through the challenges of living with a daily information tsunami.

The nine-second stat applies only to data. The minute we engage with emotion and story, a much wider window of attention opens. So it's time to move beyond binary: yes, use data, but also connect, engage and inspire with the right story. Stories earn compound interest from your audience.

ROCKET FUEL

I'm not suggesting that with one story the world will be your oyster. Nor am I saying that everything needs a story. But every time you want to persuade, compel and move an audience, a story will help you. A story combined with data is your success rocket fuel. I have seen this time and time again, with leader after leader, in large, medium and small organisations all over the world.

So besides your other practices, if you want to learn, explore and discover practical applications for business storytelling (storytelling with a purpose and for results), then you are in the right place. This is the right book for you.

Stories and storytelling can inspire, influence, motivate and engage people, where logic and bullet points may not. Think of your own experience. Isn't it always the story, the anecdote, the example that you remember long after the event?

Whatever it is you are trying to do in business – whether you are leading people, managing change, influencing the board or building your career – storytelling will help you do it better … that's a guarantee. So let our journey begin!

A good way to start is by defining what business storytelling is and what it isn't, which is what we will do in the next chapter.

KEY INSIGHTS

- Leaders face the challenges of leading a team, guiding change and inspiring others (it's about relationships and results).
- Hard power (command and control) and soft power (consulting, collaborating and connecting) are in themselves not enough as influence tools to address these three challenges.
- The currency of business has changed – the new currency is business storytelling.
- Business storytelling (storytelling with a purpose and for results) lets us fast-track relationships and results.
- The Aristotle model of influence tells us we need *logos* (logic), *ethos* (personal credibility) and *pathos* (emotional connection) to succeed.
- In business we are *logos* heavy and don't have the tools to use *ethos* and *pathos* effectively.
- Storytelling fast-tracks *ethos* and *pathos*.
- Storytelling helps us dodge the curse of knowledge.

2. WHAT IS BUSINESS STORYTELLING?

Business storytelling is storytelling with a purpose and for results.

As an example, let's look at a very old story (which I first heard when Benjamin Zander shared it in his TED talk) about two shoe salesmen from competing companies who are sent to Africa in the early 1900s to assess market opportunities. The first telegraphs his office: 'Situation hopeless. Stop. They don't wear shoes.' The other sends: 'Glorious opportunity! They don't have any shoes yet.'

The story had the audience roaring with laughter. A conductor and musical director, Zander then linked it to his own message: 'There's a similar situation in the classical music world, because there are some people who think that classical music is dying. Yet there are some of us who think you ain't seen nothing yet!' Passionate about classical music, he knew that most of his audience would probably roll their eyes at the mention of the genre. So he used the most powerful tool in the book, storytelling.

This is an example of business storytelling that is purposeful (it links to his message), is tailored to an audience and delivers results.

Is that it? Do I stop reading here? Why is there a whole book on mastery, then? Ah … if it was only so simple, my friend. It's like reading the definition of rocket science ('*Rocket science is a primary branch of aerospace engineering*') and stopping there. But we know this definition packs a tome and for many people a lifetime's experience and expertise. As with business storytelling, a simple definition conceals more than it reveals.

The surprising thing about business storytelling is that your stories do not have to be about business! That would be boring. Business storytelling, whether it involves parables like the one shared by Benjamin Zander or personal stories, is about engaging people's hearts and emotions.

IT'S SIMPLE BUT NOT EASY

The world's most successful value investor, Warren Buffett, often speaks in folksy aphorisms – I guess in modern terms that would be tweets. He famously said about investing, 'It's simple but not easy'.

Interestingly, I get more feedback on this from clients all over the world than anything else. Not about investing, but about storytelling. 'Storytelling is much harder than it looks,' they often share with me.

So, borrowing from Mr Buffett, I must tell you that storytelling is simple but it's not easy. When someone shares a story, it sounds simple, effortless even. Simplicity means you, the audience, 'get it'. You understand the story and the point it is making. Consider this gem from the late great David Foster Wallace, a brilliant American writer: 'Two young fish are swimming along and they meet an older fish, who nods and says, "Morning, boys. How's the water?" They swim on for a while before one young fish looks over at the other and says, "What the hell is water?"'

For Wallace, the point of the story is that the most obvious, ubiquitous, important realities are often the hardest to see and talk about. This is the truth about storytelling – it is obvious yet hard to do well.

When we look at Wallace's story, it's relatable. It's also short – three sentences. And in a business context, it's purposeful. These are the essential hallmarks of an effective story. They are also the features that make a story *seem* simple.

What, then, makes a story so difficult to craft?

The very features that make it simple (relatable, short and purposeful) make it hard! Catch 22.

For a story to work in business it has to be relatable, which generally means it's about people, usually a single person (never a team or organisation), that your audience can relate to. Your audience can then see themselves in the story.

Business people struggle with keeping their stories short. My rule of thumb is a story in business should be told in no more than two minutes. It takes a lot of thinking, crafting and redrafting to nail this. Why this hardline restriction? I have often told a story that took five minutes or longer, you might retort petulantly. (Your poor audience, I feel for them.) In a business setting, after two minutes your audience's attention span usually flags.

Short and sharp works best, and I'll show you how to pack a punch in just two minutes or under. Every rule has its black swans or outliers, of course. And sometimes a long story, if carefully crafted, can work. But treat these as exceptions. In business, the first skill to master is to do a short story well, so it lands on purpose with your audience.

This is perhaps the hardest thing to do well when telling a story – to land it on purpose. The power and juice of a good story lie in how you link it to a message (purpose). Story magic happens when you do so in a way that is elegant, delightful even, and not clunky. This is hard even for story ninjas.

Stories that are simple, short and purposeful are not easy to craft and deliver. And mastery definitely takes a whole book – specifically, this book!

I MIGHT ALREADY BE DOING THIS ...

Recently I was presenting on the power of business storytelling at a professional services firm. They had brought me in with the brief that the team members needed to humanise their content. Clients had been complaining about drowning in data and not feeling a connection to the solutions. Professional services team members, some clients claimed, were 'robotic' in their client interactions.

In my presentation I show why storytelling is important and I encourage participants to experience the power of storytelling and explore the missing piece in their practice. It's high energy, fun and practical (my sessions, not their practice). At the end of this presentation, one of the audience members said, 'We already do this. We have always shared stories about our work, our war stories'.

My jaw almost hit the ground! Here is what is happening when leaders think they already use storytelling.

Leaders who use storytelling are an anomaly; they are the exception rather than the rule. If you, as a leader, are using stories brilliantly, you cannot make the assumption that this is happening across the board in your company (especially when client feedback indicates the opposite).

Frankly, war stories, or stories about 'how we do things here', will often bore your clients. They are not tailored to your audience, who therefore don't invest their attention in these stories. I call this *asymmetrical storytelling*, where the audience doesn't see the story the same way the narrator does.

If you are already using storytelling in business, there is always room for improvement. Are your stories short, purposeful, crafted for an audience? Is there impact on their delivery? Are you measuring your ROIs and building your library of stories?

To help you answer these questions, I want to share my model:

When it comes to storytelling, some people are *amateurs*: they don't understand how to use it. Some are *apprentices*: they have just started learning about it. With proper skills, training and practice, some people become *masters*. They influence and make an impact with their stories. These are like black belts in karate. Finally, there are the story *artists* – think Brené Brown or Ken Robinson. They are like karate masters. Interestingly, in karate as in storytelling, even the artists never stop learning.

FIGURE 2.1: AMATEUR TO ARTIST MODEL

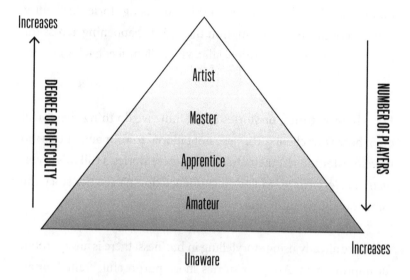

HIJACKED OR PRECIOUS?

At a recent event I introduced myself as a business storyteller, which is what I am. There was a time when no one understood what that meant. Not so today. The person next to me then introduced himself: 'I'm a storyteller too, only I tell stories with numbers.' Everyone looked confused. We later found out he was an accountant!

One part of me celebrated – the word *storyteller* is now so sexy that it's being hijacked wholesale – but another part was unconvinced.

Stefan Sagmeister, of the design firm Sagmeister & Walsh, doesn't mince words when he calls this bluff: 'I think all the storytellers are not storytellers. Recently I read an interview with someone who designs roller-coasters and he referred to himself as a "storyteller".

No, @%$#head, you are not a storyteller, you're a roller-coaster designer! And that's fantastic and more power to you … '

Until I read Sagmeister, I thought I was being precious about labels. He helped me to better understand that while we all can and should storytell – it makes what we do engaging, interesting and relevant – using storytelling as a tool and being a storyteller are two quite different things.

It's not (just) that my nose is out of joint (really!). I worry that it reflects a deeper problem. If you describe yourself as a storyteller when you are an accountant, then the first story you are sharing is spin. Not cool.

I totally get that in a fluid, agile work environment, the work we do cannot always be distilled into one or two words. Right up to the 1980s the Australian census job question asked only for your job title. Today the census features a two-part question: 'What is your title?' and 'What do you do?' Because titles like 'Chief Fun Officer' beg for more information.

So whether you are filling a census form or simply describing to someone what you do, my advice is the same. Celebrate what you do! And find a sexy way to describe it (without hijacking the word storyteller). But unless you really are a professional business storyteller, don't hijack that word!

The word *story* is being hijacked in a similar way. Often leaders imagine they are sharing stories when what they are really sharing is case studies or data. Labelling something a story does not make it one!

Storytelling and stories are sexy. So we just change the label on something, put lipstick on a pig and hope that works. There is so much language in this space, it is worth unpacking a few common terms before doing a deep dive into what storytelling is.

STORIES, NARRATIVES, METAPHORS

Harley-Davidson was all about transport. Today their narrative is around a lifestyle – 'Born to be wild'. Members upload videos (individual stories) on this. Each of these stories builds the 'Born to be wild' narrative. Very hard to do narrative purely on a meta level.

FIGURE 2.2: NARRATIVE AND STORIES

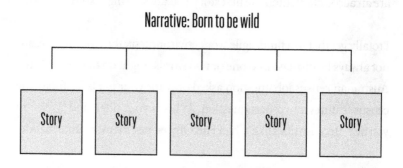

My narrative arc is this: I am a storytelling expert and I share a range of stories, from my Miss Asha story on page 26 (which shows I have been on this journey my whole life) to stories about the results my clients have had using storytelling. Every story in this arc hangs off the storytelling expert narrative.

Think of narrative as a meta tag. A narrative is made up of lots of stories. Each of these stories builds the meta narrative.

Metaphors illuminate an idea or concept for your audience. The good ones paint an evocative picture. The great Indian poet Rabindranath

Tagore described the Taj Mahal as 'a solitary tear suspended on the cheek of time'. It takes a Nobel Prize–winning poet laureate to conjure up that wonderful image.

You can and should absolutely use metaphors as part of your toolkit, though please steer clear of clichéd sports metaphors. Also, recognise the different purposes of metaphors and stories. A metaphor helps people understand, while a story moves people to action. Lori Silverman captures it well in *Business Storytelling for Dummies*, when she says, 'Case studies, examples, anecdotes are information based. Story is emotion based. Emotion comes from the Latin word to move.'

STORY ELEMENTS

In a landmark obscenity trial in 1964, US Supreme Court Justice Potter Stewart acknowledged the near impossibility of defining the legal boundaries of 'hard-core pornography', while commenting ironically, 'I know it when I see it ... ' This expression became known in legal circles as the Stewart test. In the 50 years since, the Supreme Court has continued to grapple with what constitutes 'obscene'.

The same might be said about stories: we all know or feel a good story when we hear one. Yet when we sit down to deconstruct what makes a story a story, our best efforts come to naught. This book is practical and I want to save you time and effort, so for our purposes what serves us best is to think about these three features of a story:

- Sequence
- Specific
- Emotion and sensory data.

Of course, this is by no means a complete list of story elements. Trying to define what a story is can feel like trying to nail jelly to a tree. But these three features will ground us every time.

Sequence

Stories have a beginning, middle and end. This is your classic story-telling sequence. Audiences love it and are hard-wired to respond to it, which is why so many fairy tales start with 'Once upon a time' and end with 'And they lived happily ever after'. Every parent who has tenderly tucked in a sleepy child after reading these words knows how satisfying it is. Sequence is the first marker of a story.

Be careful with sequence, though. It is seductive. The minute something has a sequence it looks like a story.

> Every story has a sequence, but everything with a sequence is not a story #StoryMastery

So what else do we need to look for?

Specific

Why are so many films about love, or the battle between good and evil, or coming-of-age stories? Because these are universal themes. Everyone can connect with them. They speak to our human condition. Universal themes resonate with all of us. The universal, Lisa Cron writes in *Wired for Story*, 'is the portal that allows us to climb into the skin of characters completely different from us and miraculously feel what they feel'.

Whether it is a Hollywood script or your next business story, the universal has to be packaged in the specific to be accessible. Specific makes it tangible for your audience. What happens to one specific person in a specific moment is where we unlock the magic of storytelling.

'A dog ate my lunch,' my client Jen tweeted recently, to no great response. Then she got specific: 'A Dalmatian ate my burrito,' and Twitter exploded! People loved it. Why? What separated those two tweets and transformed 'ho-hum' into 'ta-dah'? The magic happened when she was specific. A Dalmatian (not just any dog) and a burrito (not just a generic lunch). Being specific is the key to good business storytelling. Sharing a specific moment, event, person.

This sounds easy but trips up many business people. We are often good with the abstract and the general, yet for our story to resonate it has to be concrete and specific.

Do this exercise with me. What would you substitute for *shop*, *food* and *once*? My suggestions: *Walmart, tuna sandwich*, and *three years ago* or *when I was 10*. Notice how in each case we move from the generic to the specific.

In 1961, before a special joint session of Congress, President John F. Kennedy announced the goal, 'before this decade is out, of landing a man on the moon and returning him safely to Earth'. Very concrete and specific. Chip and Dan Heath, in their bestseller *Made to Stick*, ponder what JFK might have said had he been a modern-day CEO. Perhaps, they suggest, something abstract and generic along the lines of, 'Through strategically targeted aerospace initiatives and team-centered innovation ...'.

Being specific means sharing something people can visualise in their mind's eye. This is the key to business storytelling success.

Emotion and sensory data

Why is being specific so important? Because it does the two most powerful things in storytelling: it creates emotion (makes your audience feel something) and it paints a picture (sensory data).

You feel emotion only for the specific. And you are only able to paint a picture when you get specific.

Compare these two story beginnings:

> Last year I went overseas on holiday. Bad stuff and good stuff happened ...

> Last September I was in Paris on holiday. I got up one morning to find my passport had been stolen ...

The first is vague and uncompelling. Paris, on the other hand, will probably conjure up all sorts of specific images for the audience. And a stolen passport is something every traveller dreads, one of the worst things that could happen when on holiday. The second example creates emotion and paints a picture through its specificity. The table opposite gives further examples of converting the general to the specific. Begin by covering the right-hand column and see how you go.

FIGURE 2.3: CONVERTING THE GENERAL TO THE SPECIFIC

GENERAL	SPECIFIC
a shop, a pet	Bunnings, my dog Ace
food, weather	a tuna sandwich, a sizzling hot day
once	yesterday, three years ago
someone	My friend Jack
somewhere, interstate, overseas	Melbourne, Sydney, Paris

Sequence, specific, and emotion and sensory data. These features help us get our heads around what a story is and what it isn't. Next we'll explore how business storytelling differs from traditional storytelling.

HOW IS BUSINESS STORYTELLING DIFFERENT?

If you think of storytelling as a spectrum, then traditional storytelling sits at one end and business storytelling (storytelling with a purpose and for results) sits at the other. The two forms of storytelling differ in a few important ways. In business, we have to keep in mind the following three features (yes, another three).

Purpose

In business, your stories must have a purpose, or a point to make. Story purpose infuses your story with meaning. In the pub, with friends and family, your stories can be long-winded, rambling, and even play fast and loose with the truth. In business, though, you should never leave your audience confused or wondering. Here's an example of a purposeful story.

STORY TITLE: COMPUTER LOVE

I love Father's Day. One year when my son Christopher was six years old he came and gave me a gift he had hand-made. But I couldn't guess what it was! I said, 'Thanks Chris, but please tell me what it is'. He said, 'Dad, it's a computer. Look, here's the keyboard and the monitor'. I looked and saw all the intricate details. Yes, there was a keyboard – there was even a tiny clay mouse.

I said, 'Thank you, but why are you giving me a computer?' And he said, 'Dad because you love your computer. You are on it working every evening'. That moved me. I realised as parents and leaders we send powerful messages every day not through what we say but through what we do.

STORYTELLER: PROFESSOR STEPHEN R. ROBINSON,
RMIT UNIVERSITY

The purpose is the touchstone of business storytelling
#StoryMastery

In chapter 5 we'll talk about how you can land your stories on purpose, and do so with subtlety, not a sledgehammer.

Stories support data

In business, data is the hero. Reading this statement, you are probably rejoicing – or perhaps you're confused to see it in a book on storytelling. But I'm here to set you up for success, so I would never claim that all you need is a handful of stories.

Running my storytelling business, whenever I pitch for work, I use data. For me, that means engagement scores and evaluation results. Data could be a case study, sales figures, return on investment. I then use a handful of stories.

Wherever possible, support your stories with data. I attended a conference where a psychologist spoke about anxiety. He said, 'One in four Australians suffers from anxiety [the data point]. I remembered my first anxiety attack when I was 18.' Then he shared that story. Data point followed by story.

Not every story can be supported by data, of course. The Computer Love story opposite, for example, is a personal story that cannot be supported by data. But where data is available, you can make a data point that leads into your story.

Authentic

I'm a great fan of *Gruen* (formerly *The Gruen Transfer*), an Australian satirical panel show on the marketing industry. In one episode, they talked about how marketers take one truth and spin everything around it. And it struck me that business storytelling does the complete opposite. For your storytelling to be successful, *everything* about it needs to be authentic.

One of the first things to ensure, as Steve Denning has pointed out, is that your stories are both *factually* true and *authentically* true. Denning uses the *Titanic*'s disastrous maiden voyage to illustrate the point: it would be factually true to state that 700 passengers arrived in New York, but it would leave out rather a lot, not least that the ship sank and 1500 people died.

Also, for authenticity in business you as the storyteller need to believe in your story and its purpose – your intent needs to be authentic.

A few years ago we did some work with a leadership team who were outsourcing some of their work overseas and were looking for stories to support this move. When no stories emerged we asked them, 'Can you put your hand on your heart and say you believe this is the best thing for your company?' And they couldn't.

So unless you believe in the purpose you will not produce an authentic story.

Not everything needs a story, though. Use stories only if it is authentic to do so; otherwise just go with the data, which is just what that leadership team did. They presented the data on outsourcing their operations.

Finally, there needs to be congruence between your words and your actions. For example, you can't share stories about how you love feedback, then bite the head off the first person who offers it.

Authenticity in storytelling is everything #StoryMastery

If storytelling is so powerful, how come it is not mandated in business? Many of us still have fears that inhibit our success. In the next chapter, we will look at what holds us back and some solutions that will see us surging forward with confidence and chutzpah.

KEY INSIGHTS

- Business storytelling is storytelling with a purpose and for results.
- Storytelling is simple but not easy.
- The amateur-to-artist model plots our journey to mastery.
- The primary features of stories that help us at work are sequence, specific, and emotion and sensory data.
- Business storytelling differs from traditional storytelling in that it is driven by purpose, supported by data (where possible) and *always* authentic.

3. WHAT STOPS US?

You are giving a work presentation and you suddenly realise you're stark naked. Everyone else is fully clothed of course, and you are beyond mortified that they're going to notice at any moment that you're not. Your heart is pounding as you look around desperately for somewhere to hide … then you wake up in a cold sweat. Thank god it was only a dream!

The universality of this dream (finding yourself naked in public) across age groups, cultures and ethnicities has been fodder for psychologists for decades. They all agree on one thing: it does *not* indicate a secret desire to turn into a nudist!

Psychologist and dream analyst Ian Wallace says we select clothes to represent a certain image (no surprise there), and being naked in public speaks to our fear of vulnerability, of people seeing us for who we really are. It can also signify that we are hiding some of our feelings and talents for fear of judgement.

OUR FEARS

Being vulnerable (emotionally naked) is a primal fear. Good storytelling requires self-disclosure and vulnerability (sharing experiences when things went wrong). These are the core fears people have around storytelling.

In their bestseller *Creative Confidence*, Tom and David Kelley (the founders of IDEO) identify the scariest snake in the room as fear of failure. We all have this in common. Let's look at some other common fears and how to overcome them.

Some relate to our own perceived limitations, and some to our audiences. Leaders will tell me, 'But X only likes data and numbers', or some other variation on the 'Stories won't work with this audience' argument. As I have already pointed out, I never suggest stories should be used to the exclusion of everything else.

Beyond binary

When I pitch for work, I absolutely use hard data – engagement scores I have lifted, and evaluation results I have collected – and I also use a handful of stories (no pressure, but I need to role-model my craft and share my client's successes).

So my advice is never binary. If you have only been using data in your persuasion and it works, good for you! You are on a good wicket. But it's like clapping with one hand. Add the right mix of stories that support your data (and this book will show you how) and you will hear applause – the sound of both hands clapping … your audience!

Emotion not emotional

Storytelling is based on emotion. Business storytelling engages a small range of healthy emotions. It's not about being *emotional* – we don't want people weeping into buckets. A senior leader in a global financial institution shared how he was involved in a large-scale initiative across the organisation that focused on vulnerability and storytelling. And pretty soon it became a competition to see who had deeper war wounds in terms of crushed dreams and failure. It descended into a big, messy weep-off. That is not our goal!

Quite the opposite. We want to connect and move our audiences, but to do this in a positive way that is authentic and purposeful. For me, the benchmark against which I can test that my storytelling remains on track without veering off down self-indulgent rabbit-holes is to continually ask, 'How does this serve my audience?' If the show is all about you the storyteller, then that story should be culled immediately.

Shh, this is private …

Some worry about inappropriate disclosure. After all, this is work, business, not personal. It's storytelling, not group therapy.

People find it hard to believe that I am a deeply private person, given what I do for a living. I navigate these waters by deciding as a storyteller what I won't share – my private domain, so to speak. In chapter 4 we will explore this idea, but at this point, we are not looking for a warts-and-all biography from you. Quite the opposite, our objective is a curated list of stories crafted around purpose and dished up elegantly to serve an audience with integrity.

You have it or you don't

Another limiting factor is the widely held if quite illogical belief that as a storyteller 'either you have it or you don't'. Which really makes little sense, given that almost everything we do is learned. We never feel this of any other endeavour, whether it's becoming a rocket scientist or learning how to drive.

The growth mindset

We know the path to acquiring any new skill is learning and practice. There is no such thing as a natural-born storyteller. Granted, some people are better at it than others, just as some people are better at tennis or singing than others, but everyone can get better at it with preparation and practice. In her ground-breaking work, Stanford researcher Carol Dweck has developed the idea of the growth mindset. With a growth mindset you can expand your capabilities through effort and experience, regardless of your initial talent and aptitude. The very fact that you're reading this book strongly indicates you have a growth mindset.

Not good enough

Our biggest, bone-crunching fear is that our stories are not good enough. We are often first exposed to inspiring storytelling when we hear a motivational speaker on stage. They usually tell an epic story that involves scaling Mount Everest without oxygen or sailing around the world solo. And we know we have no hope of matching such audacity.

But interestingly, in leadership I find what works best on a daily basis is not epic stories but everyday stories. Stories about shopping at your local supermarket, or going to a restaurant with friends or dropping your kids off at school. Everyday stories work because your audience can relate to them. They can see themselves in your stories.

An epic story has your audience in passive spectator mode. They enjoy the spectacle of your story, but they are not involved in it. An everyday story, on the other hand, engages your audience differently, and more directly. They invest in your story emotionally, reliving their own experiences through yours.

> So unless you are a motivational speaker, the next time you embark on a story, unlock the power of storytelling by thinking everyday not epic #StoryMastery

THE REMEDIES

Sometimes leaders think you have to be creative to be a storyteller. Perhaps if you work in Hollywood, but business storytelling is the opposite of that. I work with you not in creating stories, but in curating your experiences into stories that work for your business audience. What makes a story work is the hook of shared experience. The more everyday your experience, the more your story is going to resonate. So common is good!

In storytelling, real wins every time. If you are authentic with your storytelling, your audience will connect with you. The philosopher/poet and my favourite bad-boy Kid Rock says, 'If it looks good you'll see it. If it sounds good, you'll hear it. If it's marketed right, you'll buy it. But if it's real, you'll feel it'.

We have lived through the era of sex (using sex to sell, that is) and spin. Now we are in a new era and rediscovering what has worked for millennia – stories. If you have a pulse and you are human, you have plenty of stories. You may not see it that way, but this is where this book and I will transform a desert into a story oasis – guaranteed.

And it is one field where doubt can be your friend. A fierce friend. Doubt around who you are to share your stories? That doubt will give your stories humility. That, rather than a swashbuckling arrogance that everyone is dying to hear your stories, is the best starting place for success. So doubting Thomases may proceed beyond this point.

In storytelling what works best is imperfection. It keeps your stories 'real' and relatable. So if you feel your stories are not perfect, take a gold star. It's the secret of their success. The mindset that frees us up is progress, not perfection.

So how do we storytell? In the next chapters we'll explore, test and learn the tools that will help us find, craft and share purposeful, compelling stories.

KEY INSIGHTS

- As storytellers, we commonly experience fears around vulnerability, being emotional, inappropriate disclosure and our stories not being good enough.
- We need to move through these fears by embracing a growth mindset and recognising that it is everyday stories not epic stories that truly connect with an audience.
- By moving forward from fear to courage, we learn that imperfection and doubt are not our bitterest enemies but our best allies.

4. FINDING STORIES

The first step in our storytelling mastery journey is to find stories from our experiences.

'But I don't have any stories. I've led the most boring life,' clients sometimes gripe. Odd as this may sound, this is actually a strength in business storytelling. In this chapter, we will learn why plainer is better with regard to stories. Stories from your ordinary, everyday experiences are highly relatable.

Everyone has these stories; if they think they don't, they're simply looking in the wrong places. So in this chapter we'll go on a story quest and unlock the secret to finding stories. Like Don Quixote, we'll see giants where others see only windmills. No, we won't become delusional and disconnected from reality, but we will see things in new ways. And then we'll see stories *everywhere*.

Stories surround us, yet mostly they remain invisible to us, like the air we breathe (remember David Foster Wallace's fish story).

We also feel under pressure to ensure that every story be original. Here we might find solace in Mark Twain's famous letter to Helen Keller in which he debunks the myth of originality. Twain wrote, 'For substantially all ideas are second-hand, consciously and unconsciously drawn from a million outside sources ... '

Now I'm *not* advocating plagiarism. I am saying that as storytellers we can draw on a million outside sources. Let's embark on a story quest, and let our mindset be (courtesy of Buzz Lightyear from *Toy Story*) 'to infinity and beyond'.

STORY QUEST

This is where we grab a pair of binoculars and head out into life (hardhat optional) looking for stories. In my master classes I use a whiteboard to brainstorm where to find them. Usually we'll get a list that looks something like this:

Business storytelling – where to find stories?

- Personal experiences
- Family, kids, holidays
- Other people's experiences
- Stuff that happens at work
- History
- Books
- Social media
- Print media
- Pop culture (movies, TV shows)
- Hobbies
- Sport*

We're looking in good places. Notice the asterisk next to sport. We all know sport has tribal allegiances, so be context sensitive. Cricket stories will go down a treat in India, Australia or the UK, while (unimaginable though this is to an ardent fan like me) they are likely to bomb in Europe or the US.

But at this point, you might scratch your head and think, shouldn't that list have just one word on it? Shouldn't it just read 'BUSINESS'?

Yawn. Sorry, I zoned out there. Looking for stories from business is very limiting. And frankly it will bore your audience – not always, but often enough to make you wary.

Huh? Sadly, the term 'business storytelling' can create the assumption that the stories themselves have to be about business. Nothing could be further from the truth! Oh, you can use stories about work, about business, but don't limit yourself to those.

My vegetarian friends went to one of Melbourne's premier restaurants and ordered the nine-course degustation menu. Much to their surprise, every course had tofu as its star ingredient. Fried tofu with vegetables, gently sautéed tofu, stir-fried tofu – you get the gist. It was all delicious, but they were up to their eyeballs in tofu. But they held on, because surely the last course (dessert) offered a glimmer of hope. Finally the waiter produced it with a flourish. It was, wait for it – tofu!

That's how your audience will feel if all your stories are about business. Even if each is a gem in itself, it's just too predictable.

Some of your stories can be about business, yours or others. Some tofu is good, or at least my vegetarian friends think so. But the truth is, most business stories (there is no polite way to say this) are boring! All is not lost, though. As you work through this book, I'll share how even business stories can be used well.

The path to story mastery, however, is paved with personal stories that draw on experiences that aren't related to work. If you use only business stories, it is hard to stand out in a crowded marketplace. Audiences are jaded, saturated with business and bored with more of the same.

A client recently told me how one of his CEOs only shared stories about Jack Welch and GE. When the CEO dropped either of these names, everyone would roll their eyes – 'Here we go again'. Sadly, that CEO (who didn't last long in the role) interpreted business storytelling much too literally.

WHY NOT JUST BUSINESS STORIES?

At a meta level business storytelling is about humanising us and making H2H (human to human) connection at work. There is no more powerful yet simpler way to do this than through personal stories. Successful storytellers occasionally use business stories, but they know always to go personal too.

I regularly publish blog posts on LinkedIn, usually about business and storytelling. I get reasonable traction, but nothing to write home about. Recently I shared a post titled '5 stand-up comedy secrets for presenters' and (reluctantly) added a video of my own stand-up comedy debut. It was six months or more before I shared this. To my amazement, the response was overwhelming. Over a 1000 views, 100 likes, comments, shares and client emails. I know these aren't Taylor Swift–level metrics, but for LinkedIn it was huge!

The minute you use stories from outside business, but link them to a business message, you will have your audience at hello. They will remember, share and even retell your stories. And that's the gold standard in storytelling.

Maybe you're scratching your head and thinking, 'I have a terrific story about playing in a band when I was 17, but how can I relate that to work?' There is a technique for doing that, a technique that explodes our impact as storytellers. It is to understand the difference between literal and lateral stories.

Literal and lateral stories

Business stories are usually literal stories. For example, if I was looking for a story on leadership, I might read something about Steve Jobs and share that literal story. There will be no doubt in anyone's head that it's about leadership. Here is a literal story on staying true to who you are that features rapper Ice Cube.

STORY TITLE: MAN IN THE MIRROR

I went to the Sydney Opera House recently to see legendary rapper Ice Cube interviewed. When asked how he stayed so grounded and true to his purpose throughout his career, he replied along the lines of 'Big crowds, red carpets, the limousines and all that s—t, don't worry about that stuff. At the end of the day, I want to be who I started off as. I want to recognise the person in the mirror at the end of the day. In my last days I want to look in the mirror and know that I can still recognise that person, and that this business or fame didn't change me to the point I didn't recognise myself'.

Such a powerful lesson on staying true to who you are.

STORYTELLER: CAITLIN STONEHOUSE, INTERNAL COMMUNICATIONS MANAGER, SBS AUSTRALIA.

A lateral story is metaphorical. When you share a lateral story, the audience doesn't know what you will land it on. The minute you take a story out of work, it becomes lateral.

If you are sharing the story of being in a band when you were 17 – first, good on you! Your street cred just skyrocketed. Straight away it's a lateral story. This is because your audience has *no idea* where it's going. Then you land it on a message that makes sense for your audience and the story. Here's one way you could use it. Let's say you want to land the story on taking up new opportunities at work.

STORY TITLE: JOSH AND THE JUNIORS

When I was 17, I had a few killer dance moves. I know you wouldn't think it to look at me now. My friend Josh was a fabulous singer. He got a few of us together, and before you know it we had started a boy band.

I was so scared at first, because my only previous singing had been in the bathroom, but Josh persuaded me to give it a go, and it was so much fun. We were invited to school halls, parties and formals. We picked up a name along the way – Josh and the Juniors. We were getting big (okay, big for the town we lived in), then Josh's family moved and the band fell apart after that. I lost touch with Josh and only recently reconnected on Facebook. He hadn't pursued his singing – he'd become an accountant! We joked about how we should do a reunion tour as Josh and the Seniors.

I'm sharing this because so often at work, we have new opportunities that sound scary. The only way to find out if you can do something is to give it a go.

ANONYMOUS CLIENT STORY

Pros and cons

Literal stories are safe and easy to use. They make the perfect starting point for most storytellers. For your audience, they are easy to follow but generally provide a ho-hum experience. You know they will make the point you mean them to, but the biggest killer of impact is predictability. Humans are problem-solving animals. We are always predicting what will happen next or three steps ahead. If the audience can predict where this is going, or guess the message or ending at the start, then they'll zone out.

Lateral stories are more engaging. There is a freshness to them, a hint of intrigue – not of the cloak-and-dagger kind, but enough mystery to keep an audience interested. They must be landed well so the message is driven home. Be sure the message links clearly to the story.

Both kinds of stories work, when delivered by a skilful storyteller, which is you once you have read this book! Bold promise.

Once you have mastered the concept of lateral, an infinite range of stories will open up. Sometimes it's hard to find a literal story to fit your purpose. Life is messy and usually won't present you with the perfect story on a silver platter. You might spend days hunting for a business story to illustrate how people have challenged the status quo. Alternatively, you could take your story quest beyond work. Think where this has happened in life, not just at work: it will open the floodgates to a river of stories, and your journey as a lateral storyteller will begin.

Literal or lateral? One kind of story is not better than the other. That's like comparing oranges and apples. They are different, and both are valuable.

> As a story master, reach for a literal or a lateral story depending on your audience and purpose #StoryMastery

Now we have an initial list of places to look for stories, and we understand the distinction between literal and lateral stories, we are well equipped to begin our story quest. There are still two giant bogeymen standing in our way, however.

Leaning back versus leaning forward

I was reading an interview with Josh Lewandowski, the lead user experience (UX) researcher for YouTube. Josh was talking about how at YouTube they had assumed all users wanted to 'lean back' and do nothing more than watch content. Their research showed that wasn't the case, in fact. Viewers looked for what Lewandowski called a 'lean forward' experience. Viewers want to be immersed and even to interact through polling.

An epic story is a 'lean back' experience for its audience; an everyday story is a 'lean forward' experience that the audience can become a part of and immerse themselves in. So unless you are a motivational speaker, the next time you embark on a story, think everyday not epic to unlock the power of storytelling.

I'm afraid of TMI

Our other biggest fear is that we might disclose too much, giving our audience too much information (TMI) when using personal experiences in our stories. Eww. At work, no one wants to be like that friend on Facebook who overshares. Oversharing can discomfit your audience or even make them cringe. The opposite of a group hug, it's a group 'awk mo' that can haunt you for a lifetime.

The paradox is that successful storytelling requires vulnerability, which begs the question, how can we step around this to do storytelling well? When working with clients, I suggest thinking in terms of 'storytelling wells'. It's from these wells that you draw your stories. The wells supply you with storytelling ideas, helping you to find the balance between vulnerability and oversharing.

Every item in our story quest list fits into the model below. The model also addresses how personal a story can be, and how to keep private stuff private.

STORY DOMAINS MODEL (STORY WELLS)

The following domains are our story wells, each unique and providing you as a storyteller with an almost unlimited resource of stories to fit your purpose:

- public domain
- professional domain
- personal domain
- private domain.

Let's now look at each of these domains in turn.

FIGURE 4.1: STORY DOMAINS MODEL

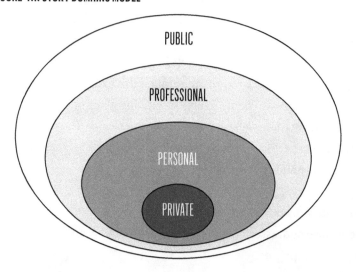

PUBLIC DOMAIN

Stories in the public domain are available to everyone. You might see something on YouTube or read a story in the newspaper. Public domain stories are not exclusive to you. Indeed they are sometimes already familiar, even if their source is unknown. Let's take the starfish story as an example. You may have heard this one at a conference, in a workshop or in another business context.

STORY TITLE: STARFISH STORY

Once upon a time, there was an old man who used to go to the ocean to do his writing. He had the habit of walking on the beach every morning before he began work. Early one morning, he was walking along the shore after a big storm and found the vast beach littered with starfish as far as the eye could see.

Off in the distance, the old man noticed a small boy approaching. As the boy walked, he paused every so often and as he grew closer, the man could see that he was bending down to pick up an object and throw it into the sea. The boy came closer still and the man called out, 'Good morning! May I ask what you are doing?'

The young boy paused, looked up and replied, 'Throwing starfish into the ocean. The tide has washed them up onto the beach and they can't return to the sea by themselves,' the youth replied. 'When the sun gets high, they will die, unless I throw them back into the water.'

The old man replied, 'But there must be tens of thousands of starfish on this beach. I'm afraid you won't be able to make much of a difference.' The boy bent down, picked up another starfish and threw it as far as he could into the ocean. Then he turned, smiled and said, 'It made a difference to that one'.

STORY SOURCE UNKNOWN

Find and capture

Finding stories in the public domain requires you to have your story lens on at all times. Scan your environment and think, what's the story here and how can I use it in business?

Sometimes the story might already present with a purpose. This example, used to describe competitive advantage, often features in MBA textbooks on strategy.

STORY TITLE: GRIZZLY BEAR

Two CEOs are spending a weekend in the woods for some bonding time. Across a clearing a grizzly bear shambles out. One of the CEOs drops his backpack and pulls out a pair of runners. The other says, 'Are you nuts? You can't outrun a grizzly bear!' To which the first replies, 'I don't have to, but I can sure as hell outrun you!' And that's competitive advantage in a nutshell.

STORY SOURCE UNKNOWN

This story is quite well known and is pre-packaged so we know how to land it on message. But often with public domain stories, you spot a great story first before you figure out how you might use it. Think of the YouTube clip from China that shows a crowd of strangers working together feverishly to lift a bus and free an elderly woman trapped beneath it. You don't know *yet* what you will do with it, but capture it first and you can decide later on how to purpose it.

I use the Evernote app and keep a notebook in there called 'A story a day', and I add one every day. (What can I say? I'm a story nerd!) Record your public domain stories or link to them, because it's surprising how you will forget them otherwise. Analogue also works well: an actual notebook and good old-fashioned pen can do the trick.

Here's a screenshot from my notebook.

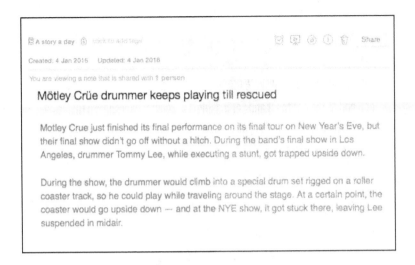

The story of the Mötley Crüe drummer playing till he was rescued was too good to let go. I don't know yet what I can use it for – could be about not letting customers down or the show must go on. I'll decide later. But if I hadn't captured that gem in some format, I'm sure I would have long forgotten it.

Cease and desist

Sometimes people try to pass off public domain stories as their own. They know personal stories pack more power, so they take something from out there and falsely claim it as their own.

This is what a facilitator shared at one of my clients' conferences.

STORY TITLE: POT ROAST

Last week I watched my wife prepare a meal. As I watched she cut off one end of the pot roast and set it aside. I asked her why she did this. She answered, 'Because my mother always cut off the end of the roast'. I was none the wiser so I went to my mother-in-law and asked her the same question. She said, 'Because *my* mother always did it that way!' I couldn't leave it there, so I went to my wife's grandmother and asked her about this strange family practice. She just laughed and said, 'I always cut off the end of the roast because I didn't have a pan big enough to fit the whole roast'. Some traditions are like that! Let's look at what we do and why we do it that way.

STORY SOURCE UNKNOWN

All the conference participants connected with the story and the message. The next day another facilitator arrived and said, 'I want to share this parable with you,' and repeated the same story, to the amazement of all the participants. The credibility of the previous facilitator was shot to pieces, because he had passed off this story as his own.

One of the participants' shared this whole experience with me, adding, 'We were so angry and didn't care anymore about the valuable stuff we had learned in the workshop. All we could remember was he had lied to us by saying this had happened to him when it was a well-known story. We wondered what else he had said that wasn't true.'

If a story is not your own, credit it. A good segue into a public domain story might be:

- I was watching a YouTube clip – some of you might have seen it. A man ...
- I want to share this story I heard in a workshop I attended recently ...
- Some of you might have heard this story ...

Credit your stories where you can and stay credible.

PROFESSIONAL DOMAIN

These are stories about things that happen at work. They could be from your employees, customers or stakeholders. A legendary customer service story comes out of Zappos, an online shoe retailer with a core value to 'deliver WOW through service'. When Zappos learned that a customer's order had been delivered to the wrong location, they delivered another pair of shoes by express at no extra charge. It so happened that the customer was best man at a wedding, and the replacement order saved the day.

Common sources for stories from your professional domain are:

- your heritage, history or founders
- employees
- customers and stakeholders.

Heritage, history or founder stories

These stories are historic and can be static. Sometimes they are already documented; sometimes they are part of the mythology of an organisation. If the founders are still in the business, interviewing them can provide fresh insights.

The graphic design company Canva presents a typical founder story on its website: 'The Canva journey began back in 2007 when Melanie Perkins was studying at the University of Western Australia. Melanie taught students how to use programs such as InDesign and Photoshop – programs that people found hard to learn and even harder to use.' The story tells of their journey, initially into school year books and later recognising that the technology had broader applications. Today Canva is a simple-to-use online design platform that allows anyone to create professional-quality designs. It is an Australian unicorn startup valued at over $1 billion.

It's good to have some heritage or history stories, but please recognise their limited value. The Canva story is contemporary; its unicorn status and the press that followed it created a buzz. But conventional heritage and history stories tend to have a narrow audience, usually limited to the people who work there (and we can't be sure they aren't faking interest for the sake of their careers). I know this isn't good news, but tough love here will help you find stories that are really interesting. Which is what we'll look at next.

Employee and customer stories

Like the Zappos story above, these are your employee and customer experiences. They are dynamic stories that most often focus on the present, the immediate past or even the future.

Are we talking war stories? Umm, no! War stories are about the good old days, how things were around here, how we did things in the past. Not all war stories are bad, but it's best to avoid them or use them sparingly. This is because war stories are an example of asymmetrical storytelling. The teller is more invested than the listener, which makes them less engaging for the listener. There's an interest asymmetry. No, what we are talking about is using current stories from your customers, employees or other stakeholders. This is harder than it sounds. Here's an example of an organisation that has nailed it.

The Ritz-Carlton way

The Ritz-Carlton is a luxury American hotel chain that consistently uses storytelling to inspire and remind employees what excellence looks like. They collect stories from employees every day.

Employees (The Ladies and Gentlemen of Ritz-Carlton) are invited to write up and share special moments, called 'Wow' stories, with head office. What is to be admired is how as many of these 'Wow' stories are about small, simple gestures as about grand and creative achievements. What qualifies a story is the care provided.

Each week two 'Wow' stories are shared during a meeting that includes every Lady and Gentleman around the world. It is just one reason, the hotel suggests, why employees feel proud to say, 'I am Ritz-Carlton.'

The Ritz-Carlton has a long history with storytelling and has steadily fine-tuned and tweaked its processes. Your organisation may not have such a sophisticated story machine that is constantly panning for and sharing employee stories. You will often have to pan for story gold yourself. And there may be barriers that impede your success.

Caution, barriers ahead

Some employees are reluctant to share their stories. In Australia, we sometimes fall victim to the tall poppy syndrome (a tendency to disparage people who achieve prominence). Some people are reluctant to blow their own trumpet. Fear of standing out, of being a 'tall poppy', can often keep us grounded but can also sometimes lock us into a false humility that stops us celebrating our success or sharing our stories.

One way around this is to have people nominate their mates! Where we may be reluctant to talk about ourselves, we are happy to share a team member's achievement or a colleague's positive customer feedback. Occasionally a participant in one of our workshops shares a work story that blows everyone out of the water, yet the sharer airily dismisses this with a shrug, saying, 'I was just doing my job'.

When people hear a workmate's story they'll sometimes exclaim, 'I've worked with you for five years. I sit less than five metres away and I didn't know that!' Most often this is because there was never a contextual opportunity in which sharing the story would have been appropriate.

Story harvesting techniques

One way of successfully navigating all these issues to help us find stories is to use story harvesting invitations. These are framing statements that help draw out stories.

Each of the following invitations is a magnet, designed to attract stories. None includes the word story, which itself can put pressure on people who think you are looking for something extraordinary.

- Share an example of when you saw a small change at work make a difference.
- Describe a time when you or someone you know at work did the right thing for a customer.
- Recall an instance when you heard a customer describe a positive experience they had with a team member.
- Share a time when you felt proud to work here.
- Tell us about a time when you or someone you know delivered a great customer experience.
- Share a time when you or someone you know had positive feedback from a customer, colleague or stakeholder.
- Give us an example of something you have seen or heard recently at work that inspired you.
- Describe a time when someone at work shared a positive experience.
- Share a time when our organisation has done the right thing (by you, a colleague or the community).
- Share a time when you went home excited about something that happened at work.

I use a bespoke version of this tool to run story harvesting sessions for my clients. I have to tailor it to suit each client and their context to find the kinds of stories they are looking for. For example, it might be given an innovation or implementation slant. This tool is most successful with people who work at the coal face.

At the end of a story harvesting session, most people feel re-energised and excited about where they work. I recently ran a series of sessions at a leading financial institution that generated an out-pouring of stories. A participant said at the end, 'for the first time in three years I feel proud to work here.'

Customers are no longer satisfied with just being told a story; they want to feel part of the story. Brands like Red Bull encourage customers to post videos.

The professional domain can be a rich treasure trove of stories.

PERSONAL DOMAIN

At this well we draw on personal experiences for stories to share. Personal stories bring the rich texture of our personal lives into the workplace while linking each story to a business message. They are powerful in business, but they do require a level of self-disclosure and vulnerability.

If it's business, make it personal

'It's not personal, Sonny, it's strictly business' is a famous line from the 1972 film *The Godfather*. In the business world, this is a common myth we have been raised on. To succeed as business communicators, it's time to challenge that notion. If you want your messages to stick, if you want to have an impact as a leader and to be a storyteller extraordinaire, break with conventional wisdom and use personal stories to land a business message.

A few years ago we did some work with the chair of a global multinational whose message was 'spend company money as if it is your own' – in other words, be careful how you spend company money. This sounds like just another trite company line about cost-cutting. We asked him how he was going with this message and he replied candidly, 'Not great, but I'm going to keep banging on about this until it hits home.' We asked him why.

He replied that when he was growing up, his parents were not poor, but neither were they wealthy. Both his parents worked very hard and worked full time. His mum always told him you work hard for your money but you get to spend it only once, so spend it wisely.

Once we discovered he had never shared this story with his team, we invited him to do so the next time he was presenting this message. He began with the story and then linked it to the message by saying that was why 'spending company money as if it is our own resonates with me'.

He was surprised at the connection this personalisation created and how the behaviour around spending company money changed. People realised he was genuine about the message and not just pushing yet another company line.

Success and failure stories

We often fall into the trap of picking personal stories that show us in the best light (success stories). We're only human, after all. Success stories are important, but they should not be the only stories in your personal domain.

A consulting client was involved in a multi-billion-dollar pitch. They were presenting after two other consulting companies. At the end of the pitch, the decision makers said to them, 'All three of the consultancies who pitched today have been vanilla. Instead of always telling us how amazing your work is, can you share a time when things *didn't* go to plan and how you recovered?'

The pitch team was immediately dumbstruck. This was a group of intelligent, articulate, smart professionals. The client was looking for failure stories, and of course they had dozens of them, but nothing they could pull out under the spotlight and under pressure.

But why? What can be better than a success story?

Success stories are great, but failure stories are even better. Robert Kaplan of Harvard Business School tells us failure stories are defining. The only way your audience can know who you are as a leader and a person is by reflecting on your failures and how you handled them. 'Both wins and losses define your path forward.' Kaplan advises writing up your failure stories, focusing on the traumas and setbacks in your life. Failure stories are highly relatable. We have all been there – it's part of the human experience. But always temper your failure stories for your purpose or audience, and avoid the 'poor me' approach.

The struggles in failure stories are connected not to skill but to doubt. There is a fine line between incompetence and humility. We all get it when an accountant struggles with work–life integration. Managing a busy work and personal life is never easy. But an accountant who shares how they stuff up the numbers – whoa, our empathy vanishes! That sounds like incompetence. The right failure stories, though, add texture, depth and variety to our storytelling craft. After working with me, this consulting client articulated their failure stories with impact and on message.

Risky business

Personal stories immediately engage a business audience, but they take skill and confidence. Finding the right personal story that serves our purpose and our audience can be challenging.

We feel vulnerable when we share personal stories, yet we know instinctively that they pack a punch. These stories pressure test our risk capacity. They feel perilous but, with the right business storytelling training they need not be.

As in life, the greater the risk, the greater the reward.

Here's a client example.

STORY TITLE: BOXING AND THE MONK

When I was a teenager, as an elite athlete in New Zealand I started to study under a monk. On the very first day he asked me to box without gloves. I had to punch a boxing bag until he commanded me to stop. Being young and enthusiastic I went for it and punched the bag, hard. Within seconds the raw pain kicked in and in 30 seconds I wanted him to yell stop. I looked at him and nothing, my knuckles were raw and I could see blood.

The pain was numbing and then suddenly I found I had flow. I got into a rhythm and didn't feel the pain anymore. The monk then called out stop and I fell to the ground.

Lying on the floor, clutching my hands, through the mist of pain, I realised that more powerful than the body is the mind.

STORYTELLER: EX-NZ
INTERNATIONAL CRICKETER

> Story masters know the power of business storytelling rests with personal stories #StoryMastery

More power to the personal!

PRIVATE DOMAIN

The private domain contains the stories you decide **not** to share. Each storyteller must decide what is private for them. While powerful storytelling requires vulnerability and sharing, it's important we don't regret sharing some of our stories.

After all, this is business. Business storytelling taps into healthy emotions, without necessarily getting emotional. Causing people to weep is not a hallmark of success.

Also, it is important that your stories work for your audience. I was at a conference where one speaker mentioned being abused (without giving any detail). The audience was shaken by this revelation. The speaker had opened a door into a dark place but had not closed it. People were disturbed and couldn't see the purpose of that throwaway line.

Sometimes a presenter may choose to share a personal story about their struggle with a serious illness, such as cancer. The test I recommend my clients use is: how does this serve the room – that is, how does it help your audience? If you're unsure about just where to draw the line between personal and private, this simple test can help.

Understanding and using the storytelling wells outlined in this chapter will prevent you from floundering on the rocks of inappropriate disclosure. Exploring these wells on your story quest will help you build up a story treasure to share.

Now, before moving on, choose a story idea from any of the domains identified. It doesn't have to be the perfect story, just an idea. The following chapters show you how to structure it for success. The first step after finding a story (using the tools in this chapter) is to give it a purpose. That's what we will look at next.

KEY INSIGHTS

- Your story quest begins by compiling a conventional list of story sources.
- Understanding the difference between literal and lateral stories opens up new sources of stories.
- These story wells will never run dry.
- The four story 'domains' / 'wells' are the public domain, the professional domain, the personal domain and the private domain.
- Understanding the domains helps you get the balance right between vulnerability and over-sharing.
- They'll also give you a bottomless treasure chest of potential stories.

5. THE POWER OF PURPOSE

STORY TITLE: PASTA AND OUTPUTS

One afternoon when I was five, my sister (who is older than me) asked me to make lunch because she was busy. She said, 'Just add pasta to water for five minutes, then add pasta sauce and some salt'. I made the dish following her instructions and proudly called her to the table. On the table she saw: uncooked pasta in a bowl of water, with sauce floating on top. I was standing by with the salt shaker in my hand, ready for the final flourish ... We ended up having takeaway pizza for lunch that day!

In life and in business, our input determines the quality of our output.

STORYTELLER: ALESSANDRO CARONTI, TRANSPORT ACCIDENT COMMISSION (TAC)

The purpose of this story by Alessandro Caronti is found in the last line: output depends on input. In business, our stories must have a purpose. If you take away the last line (the purpose), it's just a charming anecdote. Add purpose and – *kapow!* – it explodes with impact.

The purpose is the point of the story, the message the story conveys. Children's fables often end with the line, 'And the moral of the story is ...' To use such language in business would sound patronising and self-righteous. I'll show you some more nuanced and sophisticated ways to share your purpose.

Remember, purpose lands your story on message. It creates meaning for your story. It's the key difference between business storytelling and traditional storytelling (what we do in the pub, with friends and family). In business, a story without a purpose is like a boat with no oars. You'll bob about on the seas of life, but you're unlikely to get where you want to go. You might like bobbing about, but your audience who are in the boat with you will be clenching their jaws and wondering when it will ever end. With business storytelling, you never want to leave your audience thinking, 'What was the point?'

> Purpose gives your story a destination, the place you want to land your story #StoryMastery

STAND FOR SOMETHING

For the storyteller, purpose compels you to stand for something. There's nothing fluffy or wishy-washy about a great story. The best stories are anchored by purpose.

Purpose helps us stand for something. Challenged in an *AFR* article about claims that Starbucks' standard-blend coffee has a burnt flavour, former CEO Howard Schultz responded, 'We don't apologise for it, we love it. And 100 million customers last week – 100 million – said that they like it too.'

I'm not saying injecting purpose will polarise your audience or stop your story from being broadly popular. What it will do is ensure you're not trying to be all things to all people, and ending up catering for the lowest common denominator.

Purposeful storytelling is powerful storytelling. #StoryMastery

Story audiences look for meaning. The message or purpose of your story provides it. A story can mean different things to different people, but you as storyteller decide what purpose and meaning to invest it with. In the pasta story, Alessandro Caronti lands it on how your inputs determine your outputs.

PEDANTIC ON PURPOSE

I'm pedantic about purposeful business storytelling. I believe a story without a purpose is a missed opportunity. Why?

Purpose lands the story for both storyteller and audience. It helps bring your audience home, rather than leaving them scratching their heads and wondering what that was all about. Otherwise, it's like being in a plane that circles and circles without landing. Even those travelling in the luxury of first class will tire of it eventually, and when it runs out of fuel it will be forced to make an emergency landing.

A story with a clear purpose sorts the masters from the amateurs. Amateurs can share amusing, rambling stories, but with no purpose they may leave their audience befuddled. Story masters use purposeful storytelling to connect, engage and inspire.

When he was CEO of National Australia Bank, John Stewart was well known as a storyteller. Today, more than a decade after he left the bank, people still remember and share his stories. They are part of his legacy. With every story you tell, you leave your mark on your organisation and the people you work with.

The big picture view

Let's look at how you get going with purpose. Before picking a purpose for our stories, you need to understand a few principles and how strategy and story differ.

Story has become such a sexy word that everything carries the label. Yesterday I was watching a weather report on TV and the anchor said, 'Let's look at the weather story.' *Please!* A client showed me a strategy document across which someone had written boldly, 'Retail Strategy Story'. Word substitution is not much of a trick if the result is plain wrong. Then it's simply word appropriation. I know, but I feel strongly about this.

So here's a handy contrast frame that spells out how strategy differs from story.

FIGURE 5.1: STRATEGY VERSUS STORY

STRATEGY	STORY
Meta	Micro
Context	Content
Big picture	Specific
Abstract	Concrete
Conceptual	Practical
Jargon	Jargon free
Not always relatable	Relatable

Let's look at an example. A university might set the following strategy:

> 'To be the number one centre for learning for students
> and teachers.'

The strategy statement will then spell out how the university will achieve this – the key milestones and measures for success. The stories around this strategy will be everyday examples of what teachers and students are doing that supports the strategy.

A robust strategy will focus on the higher (meta) view of an organisation's ambitions and objectives, and is more often conceptual than specific. Organisational strategy documents are sometimes jargon-laden, and they simply will not be relatable if the 'audience' are unable to connect the dots on how their job and what they do daily ties in with the strategy.

The strategy can sometimes be aspirational – about what we will do and be 'one day'. The energy behind a strategy is as a thinking document.

A story is, on every level, the opposite of this. In our context, a story is a micro-moment (think of the pasta story in this chapter). A business story is concrete and practical; it is not an abstraction in someone's head.

To be good at storytelling in business, our stories must be jargon-free. This is non-negotiable.

Jargon is story poison #StoryMastery

A good story is specific, explicit, usually focusing on a single character, all of which makes it very relatable. Your audience see themselves in your story, and they *feel* it, because the story's appeal is not so much to our head as to our heart and emotions. Understanding this distinction is the key to nailing your story purpose.

The human touch

Nuno Assis shared photographs (mostly of buildings) on Instagram in 2012 to escape from his day job as an architect. He quickly built up a following on Instagram.

He explains his success like this: 'I like to capture moments. This could be a person hurrying through a space, a reflection of my hand in a puddle … these elements stir the viewer's imagination, more than a photo showing them what a place looks like.' Nino knows adding these elements makes a space more human and helps people relate to it.

Your purpose too, when you think about it, write it, craft it, must have a human touch. Compare these two examples:

'I want the team to deliver on executional excellence.'

Not good. What does the jargon 'executional excellence' mean? Look at the next version to see how we can nail purpose by giving it a human touch.

'In everything we do I want my team to do their best.'

This example humanises your purpose. People can relate to it, which means it will be easier to find a story for.

With story purpose, you always go micro, go human, to something you can feel and touch.

When deciding on the story message, the biggest problem I see is over-ambition. We are greedy and want to end world hunger with one story. Though storytelling is powerful, nothing is that powerful. But you can solve your own organisation's problems, one story at a time.

Let's get micro

To find the best stories you need to get to the right level of detail for our purpose. I call this *going micro* with your purpose.

The 'nail your purpose' model below offers a metaphor for finding our story purpose at the micro level, as it zooms in from the universal to the personal.

FIGURE 5.2: NAIL YOUR PURPOSE MODEL

DRILLING DOWN	METAPHOR FOR EACH STAGE
Level 1: Changing the culture **in my organisation**	Saving the world
Level 2: Changing the **sales culture** in my organisation	Saving all the children in the world
Level 3: Changing the sales **culture in my team**	Saving the children in Africa
Level 4: Getting my team to share sales information	Saving one child

At the top levels, the purpose is too broad and inclusive. The organisational equivalent of trying to save the world is yearning to change your organisation's entire culture through one story. Mission impossible!

The next level down might be to change not the whole culture but, say, the sales culture. A slight improvement on the previous purpose, but not micro enough yet.

You might then drill down into your story purpose to focus on changing the sales culture of your team. Finally (at the level equivalent to saving one child), you could make your story purpose getting the team to share sales information.

So how do you get to that level? Does it feel like smoke and mirrors, or a story ninja moment? You get there by asking a simple question.

ASK THE RIGHT QUESTION

The quickest, and smartest way to get to your story purpose fast is by asking the following question:

What is the one thing I want people to think, feel or do differently?

This question alone will get you to the micro level you need for a story purpose. By the time you have identified what you want people to think, do or feel differently, you will probably have identified quite a few things, each of which merits a story. This is illustrated opposite.

FIGURE 5.3: IDENTIFYING STORIES FOR MESSAGES

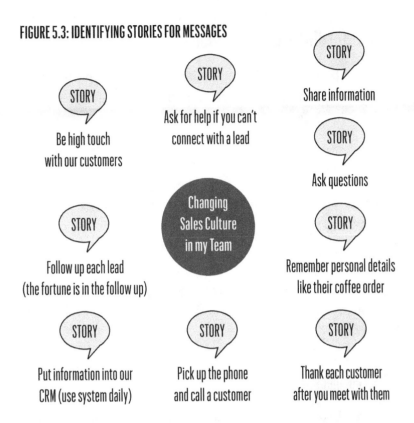

Using this approach checks the temptation to create a magnum opus of one story packed with all these points. You are not Cecil B. DeMille, and in business that kind of epic doesn't work. In business think of a series of stories, each making a point that link to overall message.

Here are examples of business purposes used in this book:

- The quality of your inputs determines your output.
- We have the power to pick ourselves up and keep going.
- Don't sweat the small stuff.
- Sometimes you have to slow down to speed up.
- Our actions speak louder than words.

REFINING YOUR STORY PURPOSE

Once you have identified several things you want people to think, feel or do differently, *pick one* and work through the next steps. The work has just begun.

Think in tweets

When you are thinking and writing up your story purpose, a good strategy is to think in tweets. Restricting yourself to 140 characters forces you to be concise and not ramble. I know Twitter itself has upped its limit to 280 characters but what can I say, I'm old school and believe brevity is the key with story purpose. I'll give you the joy of designing your own hashtag. What would your hashtag be?

Write a bumper sticker

Once you have created your tweet, you can go further and reduce your purpose to a bumper sticker. The bumper sticker doesn't have to be original or particularly sexy. You won't be printing off bulk quantities and flogging them on the open market.

You never see 'Optimising synergies' on a bumper sticker. The bumper sticker forces you to prioritise what's important to you and to express your purpose with clarity in a way that will be memorable.

Test

Now test your purpose against the 'Nail your purpose' model on page 89. Will it fit snugly in level four (saving one child)? Have you crystallised it as both a tweet and a bumper sticker? If so, you are ready to find a story for your purpose. Once you are crystal clear on purpose you've done the hardest part.

It's worth doing the hard yards with purpose, as then your story will pop easily. I have found that if clients cannot find a story or the right story, it's usually because they are fuzzy about the purpose. It's like getting reading glasses with the wrong prescription. Nothing looks good. But the minute you pop on glasses with the right magnification – *voilà*, the whole world looks bright and gleaming with possibility. That's what being clear on purpose is like.

NAILING IT

Here are some practical considerations to keep in mind with purpose. If you haven't yet nailed your story purpose, the problem usually lies somewhere here.

Jargon-free zone

When doing your washing, have you ever run a load of whites in which one rogue red item was hiding, and found it was enough to discolour the whole load? Even one drop of jargon in your purpose will make it hard for you to find a story. Jargon is toxic for purpose and for stories. Compare 'I want people to optimise synergies' with 'I want people to share information'. The minute you take out any jargon, buzzword, gobbledygook from your message, your purpose will fizz like a glass of champagne.

Turducken is purpose toast

Turducken is a dish comprising a deboned chicken stuffed into a deboned duck, further stuffed into a deboned turkey. Sometimes we can stuff a purpose with other purposes. It is hard or impossible to find a story that works in a turducken sense, as it will inevitably confuse your audience.

Wishy-washy no more

One of my clients wanted a story for 'Change is coming'. This vague, indeterminate purpose doesn't merit a story. Put on your behavioural hat to outline just what you want your audience to think, feel and do differently to move to the level you need to nail purpose.

Easy does it

As your first foray into the world of business storytelling, this is not the time to embark on your most complex, ambitious purpose. Don't bite off more you can chew. Start off modestly, practise, and before you know it you'll be nailing that ambitious, complex story too.

HIGHLY RECOMMENDED

Planning a recent trip to Japan with one of my clients, I was flicking through the *Lonely Planet* guide, in particular a section in which they highly recommend a few top sights and places to eat. So here is my version for purpose.

1. **Decide on a purpose (it's not optional).** I have said it before and cannot stress it enough. Purpose is the key to your success as a business storyteller. There is zero tolerance for purpose-free stories.

2. **Keep it short and sharp.** The purpose has to be punchy. If you need to take a big breath in mid delivery, it's too long. Long purposes don't work because they lack clarity and show the storyteller hasn't prioritised. If you've conned yourself into thinking, you can take out two purposes with one shot, you'll end up missing both. Short and sharp works every time.

3. **Believe in your purpose.** This is about your mindset. Sometimes I'm with a client and we've ticked all the purpose boxes, and there's still something missing, a barrier beneath the surface. All of this works only if you as the storyteller have conviction around your purpose. Madonna famously said, 'You have to believe you are a rock star before anyone else will.' Be rock solid in your belief, shun hedging bets and half measures.

4. **Be ready to pivot.** Sometimes you might go round and around with your purpose, refining, crafting, improving, until every day feels like Groundhog Day – and it still isn't working. Sometimes you have to be ready to let go and try something else. Then, when you have experienced the sweet taste of success, maybe you can come back to this gnarly chestnut and give it another crack.

5. **Make it relatable to your audience.** Make sure the purpose nails it not just from the storyteller's point of view, but from the audience's. Confront your biases by going back to that essential question: what do you want your audience to do differently?

KEY INSIGHTS

- The purpose is the point of the story, the message the story conveys.
- Purpose lands your story on message.
- Story audiences look for meaning. The message or purpose of your story provides it.
- With purpose, you always go micro, go human, to something you can feel and touch.
- The quickest way to nail purpose is to ask, 'What is one thing I want my audience to think, feel or do differently?'

6. START WITH AUDIENCE

'If a tree falls in a forest and no one is around to hear it, does it make a sound?' This well-known philosophical riddle raises a question about the link between existence and perception. I'm not sure of the answer (the jury is still out), but I can categorically state that if you tell a story, but no one hears it, then you don't qualify as a storyteller.

Every storyteller needs listeners – an audience. There's a beautiful symmetry here: stories need both tellers and listeners. Like a see-saw you need two people to play; one person on a see-saw is just sad. To paraphrase a line from the movie *Jerry Maguire*, the audience completes you ... or your story.

To be a story master you must always start by considering your audience. This sounds obvious., but the hard truth is we most often only pay lip service to the notion. At no time does audience matter more than when you design your story. Starting with your audience in mind makes the difference between guaranteed success and a dud.

HOW DOES THIS SERVE THE ROOM?

At a recent networking event, I met an entrepreneur who had set up a new business. When I quizzed him on his target audience, he replied wryly, 'Anyone with a pulse, really!'

In storytelling, as in business, that is a sure-fire way to bomb. Design every story with an audience in mind. Will it be your customers, your channel partners or your suppliers? How does your story serve them?

None of this is easy to do. Often as storytellers we make the mistake of starting with how a story serves *us* – our purpose, our message, our ambition. With every story we must always ask, how does this serve the room (the audience)? Starting with our audience guarantees that our story will resonate.

Rock stars can get this wrong. A few years ago U2 released their latest album on iTunes – it was added automatically, free of charge, to all iTunes users' libraries globally. Yet far from sparking gratitude, it triggered a flood of complaints. In a Facebook session in which he apologised for their presumptuousness, Bono said the move was 'a drop of megalomania, a touch of generosity and a dash of self-promotion and deep fear that these songs we poured our life into mightn't be heard'.

Bono's apology worked because of its honesty, vulnerability and humanity (yes, rock stars can get it wrong too). His mistake was not thinking about us, his audience, and making assumptions about what we would like or want. Surely nobody would say no to a free song? But we did. And yet we still love you, Bono.

The story success mindset invites us always to ask ourselves:

How does this story serve the room? #StoryMastery

Why does this matter?

When my daughter was young we used to attend the weekly tiny tots storytelling sessions at our local library. The first time I entered the room with my two-year-old, a scene of chaos, confusion and colour greeted us. Kids of various sizes were tearing up the room with boundless enthusiasm. The noise alone would have felled an elephant!

Suddenly a gong rang to announce the start of story time. It was like a magic wand had been waved. The noise dropped away. In a moment every one of the children was sitting cross-legged on the floor as the librarian opened the first book. It was a joy to see their expectant little faces, upturned noses and shining eyes as they savoured every word, often squealing with delight or laughing out loud. It was the longest I had ever seen two-year-olds stay still and absorbed.

Humans are hard-wired for both storytelling and story listening, and research shows this hard-wiring starts in children as young as two. This is how they make sense of the world, and create and share meaning. Their first story might be something like, 'Birdie fell. Cat ate Birdie!' But it is the start of their journey.

If in our overstimulated world our attention span for data has dropped to a mere nine seconds, yet when we engage with emotion and story a much wider window of attention opens up. This is because for once we are not fighting deep human conditioning but harnessing it. As storytellers, we can open this window of attention even further by tailoring the story to our audience. In old advertising language, we answer our audience's WIIFM (what's in it for me?) question.

WIIFM is a fundamental question we must return to time and time again. Getting the basics right can make us pop as storytellers, but we have to go deep with understanding our audiences.

Living in their skin

In the 2003 comic fantasy *Freaky Friday*, a mother and daughter, played by Jamie Lee Curtis and Lindsay Lohan, switch bodies after a magical fortune cookie moment. As the comedy of errors unfolds they discover the truths and lies in each other's life and get to live, breathe and experience life in each other's shoes (and body).

This would be my fantasy for every storyteller: that we literally inhabit the bodies of our audience and see life from their perspective. Where do you get those fortune cookies again? Of course it's a creepy idea and quite undoable. At the end of the film, an act of selflessness sees the magic reversed and – phew! – mother and daughter are back in their own bodies and lives.

Without getting all Buddhist on you, selflessness or empathy is the lens though which we need to view our audience. Look, observe and understand with compassion.

One of my clients makes sure people in his organisation have the help they need in terms of coaches, counsellors and psychologists. The organisation set up a confidential Employee Support Service to provide free access to an array of mental health professionals. My client spent time, effort and energy in promoting the service, getting stakeholders on board and communicating its availability. But there was little uptake of the services.

Then he thought about it from the audience's perspective, and he realised that there was a stigma attached to using the services, and that they had long-term work to do to overcome it. In many countries the discourse around mental health is slowly changing, but sadly the stigma still exists. My client recognised they were looking at generational change, so he shifted his initial focus. He changed his strategy to a simple first step: 'Pick up the phone and make a confidential call. It can change your day.'

As storytellers, this is our ambition: to see life from our audience's perspective. Sometimes we might already know our audience well. For example, leaders presenting to their peers will know their audience intimately. Yet it's not always safe to make assumptions, even if we and our audience inhabit the same world.

Regardless of how well we think we know our audience, we need to get forensic. Not in a 'stalking' kind of way. Checking on Facebook or randomly liking a few LinkedIn posts does not qualify. We need to adopt a storyteller's version of *psychographics*, the study of people according to their attitudes, aspirations and other psychological criteria. Market researchers use this sophisticated technique, in which the key data-gathering method is asking people! Face-to-face interviews. In storytelling we can use a humbler, simpler variant.

GETTING TO KNOW YOU

Our psychographics starts with exploring the 'getting to know your audience' model. This model has three levels: bronze (where you start), silver (a level up) and gold (story mastery). As we move up through these levels, we become more sophisticated as storytellers and progress from knowing our audience to understanding them, and ultimately to metaphorically becoming them. No magic fortune cookies involved.

The shift in perspective between understanding an audience and becoming the audience sees the audience moving from thinking 'you get us' (our frustrations, our joys) to 'OMG you are one of us'. It may be subtle, but the difference can be like that between water and wine.

FIGURE 6.1: GETTING TO KNOW YOUR AUDIENCE MODEL

FOCUS	I KNOW YOU	I UNDERSTAND YOU	I AM YOU
GOLD	Test	Inspiration	Bespoke
SILVER	Narrow	Aspiration	Curate
BRONZE	Identify	Fears	Context
FOCUS	WHO	WHAT	HOW

This model steps us through the three fundamental questions:

- Who is our audience?
- What do they want?
- How can we deliver this?

It is a perspective that is as close to selflessness as we are going to get in business!

Empathy underpins this model. A story from *The Age* offers a fine illustration.

Jason Russell, a volunteer with Anglicare, took a group of police on a walking tour in Fitzroy, inner-city Melbourne. Russell, who had himself once been homeless, wanted to give the police a first-hand view and understanding of homelessness. Constable Lachlan Heffernan, one of the police officers who took part, explained. 'With knowledge comes empathy and that ability to do more to help.'

As story masters, we need to bring a similar level of empathy and understanding to our audiences, otherwise the process is merely mechanical and our story will be transactional rather than transformational.

Who?

The getting to know your audience model begins with identifying who your audience is. Getting the basics right gives us the inside lane in any race. Richard Cornish, a columnist for the Epicure section of *The Age*, the foodie bible in Melbourne, shared this delightful story: 'I was in a bar in Seville and had the most sensational pickled peppers – they are like long red capsicums. Juicy and smoky, they were sensational. I asked the chef how he cooked them. He said, "I get my wife to open the tin!"'

Sometimes basic is best! At the simplest level, we ask, who is the audience for this story? It could be a single team member, your internal team or a group of suppliers. This is storytelling 101.

We might have identified a broad segment at this point. The next level requires us to narrow our focus. Think of Google Earth and zooming down into country, city, suburb and finally street view. The paradox is that the more narrowly you identify your audience segment, the more compelling your story will be. The second part of this paradox is that the more specific a story to an audience segment, the more widely relatable and universal it is.

Shashi Tharoor, an Indian politician, former diplomat, author and brilliant orator, recalled meeting an African diplomat who told him how much his African mother, who didn't speak a word of English or Hindi, loved watching Bollywood films. Every week she would make the trek to the local cinema and spend hours watching a film in Hindi and set in India, a country she had never visited. When Tharoor expressed his surprise, the diplomat explained, 'Love and romance are universal languages'.

In a commercial world dominated by mass marketing, this may sound counterintuitive.

For broad appeal, go narrow with your audience segment
#StoryMastery

Test your story on a member of your audience. If I am presenting to financial advisers, I'll have a coffee with my own financial adviser and share the stories I am planning to use. It can be confronting, but his feedback ensures I have story gold. Or someone to blame, should the stories not work out. Just kidding – they always do!

What?

Success in the 'who' stage means you have identified and understood your audience, narrowed your focus and tested your story. Next you'll move into the 'what' stage, where you uncover your audience's fears, aspirations and inspirations.

To establish their fears, you need to ask what is stopping them from taking the action you want them to take? For example, what's stopping them from sharing information right now? Is it fear of not being credited? Is it because they are time poor?

What would make them want to change, to share information? Would it be getting credit for their knowledge? A sense of achievement? Are their aspirations and inspirations big enough for them to want to reach out and overcome their fears?

This is a powerful exercise. We worked on storytelling with the head of a global organisation. Their new strategy was about taking their organisation from number four to number one in their industry. This was very exciting for the executive team. The whole strategy roadshow was built around this mother lode. Yet when the leaders did this exercise they discovered that people at the coal face didn't give a toss about being number four or number one. They cared about two things: Will this make my job easier? Will it help me serve customers better?

The leaders took this insight on board and completely changed the road-show to reflect these themes. Often the head of strategy would start the road show with, 'This new strategy will help make our jobs easier and also help us serve our customers better'. *Wham!* She had their attention.

So the two questions for you to brainstorm are:

- What is stopping them right now from [insert story purpose/ message here]?
- What would make them want to [insert story purpose/ message here]?

I have learned that clients often find it harder to identify their audience's aspirations and inspirations than their fears, yet aspirations and inspirations are more critical, because unveiling them will help you find the right emotional hot buttons to push in your story. Getting this right can reveal a green button you can hit reliably and consistently for decades, as Dove's Campaign for Real Beauty has shown.

Launched worldwide by Unilever in 2004, the Dove campaign broke with tradition by featuring everyday women, not models. The campaign celebrated women of different sizes and shapes. It demonstrated an understanding of women that was both insightful and authentic. That's what understanding our audience's hopes and dreams can do for us as storytellers.

How?

The 'how' stage helps us metaphorically 'become' our audience. We start by understanding their context, then we curate a story for their context, and finally we design a bespoke story just for them.

Context

Australian television writer and author Debra Oswald is best known for the blockbuster TV series *Offspring*. In a recent radio interview, she described how one of her first breaks was writing the TV soap *Sweet and Sour* in the 1980s. The show featured a rock band, but the writers were under strict instructions to show no drugs, no excessive alcohol and no sex, because it was a children's show broadcast at 6pm! Debra had to convince the audience this was a realistic version of the life of a rock band. To do this successfully required her to climb inside the heads of her audience of 14-year-old teenage girls. To totally get their context. This is the first step in our journey of getting to know our audience.

Curate

At the silver level we curate the story for our audience's context. Sometimes, by tailoring the content or messages, we can make the same story work for different audiences. Generally, though, curating means handpicking the right story for the audience, and making it come alive within their context.

One of my clients spoke of how his deep concern for the environment was sown at a very young age. As a young boy, his favourite book was Dr Seuss's *The Lorax*, a cautionary fable about corporate greed and environmental destruction. In the story, a young boy named Ted lives in the walled city of Thneedville, where everything is artificial and even the air is a commodity. Ted hopes to win the heart of his dream girl, Audrey. When he learns of her wish to see a real tree, Ted seeks out an old recluse called the Once-ler, a ruined businessman who lives outside of town in a stark wasteland. Ted finds out what happened to the trees, and the story ends with hope when the Once-ler gives the boy the last seed and urges him to grow a forest from it.

My client shares this and his own love for trees. It's a beautiful, heart-warming story, and was curated perfectly for his audience, who were passionate about the environment.

Bespoke

Creating a bespoke story means creating a story from scratch just for this audience.

At a pharmacy conference I attended recently I watched a presentation by a senior manager. While she herself was still young, she wanted her audience to feel how difficult the pharmacy experience was for some of their elderly clients. She donned a wig, a knee brace, glasses and a hearing aid and came in and did a role play on stage, pretending to go into a pharmacy where she couldn't hear the assistant, and both ended up shouting at the top of their voices. She had everyone in stitches, but they totally got the message. This senior manager created a bespoke story that homed in straight to her audience's work context. They all became part of the story and could see themselves or their clients in it.

AVOIDING TEMPTATIONS

As storytellers we might be tempted to take a shortcut with our audience analysis, and sometimes that's fine, but most often it's not. We might slave away on getting every story element right, practise till we are word perfect and deliver with aplomb. Yet the story will misfire if it's not grounded on the rock of understanding your audience. Michael Jordan says, 'If you try to shortcut the game, the game will shortcut you'.

When seeking to inhabit our audience it is essential to seek out and eliminate our own biases. I love chocolate and green tea (I know, go figure), but I cannot assume my audience will too. That would be projecting what I like onto my audience. So often we love one of our stories. It's superb, it always gets us a laugh and we become very attached to it. Then projection bias kicks in: we share it with the wrong audience.

The getting to know your audience model can help us every time, even when presenting to the same audience. Sometimes hubris kicks in and we go in assuming we know this audience, yet the tectonic plates might have shifted in their world.

In the BBC's cult comedy series *The Office*, shot in mock documentary style, Ricky Gervais as regional manager David Brent is an anti-hero. Brent is always out of step with his audience. It makes for great TV but would appal in real life.

In our quest for story mastery we must un-Brent ourselves! Master storytellers always need to have their finger on their audience's metaphorical pulse.

Next we will unpack 'beginnings', and how to start your stories so you hook your audience's attention.

KEY INSIGHTS

- Stories need both tellers and listeners. The audience completes you ... or your story.
- Design every story with an audience in mind. Starting with your audience in mind makes the difference between guaranteed success and a dud.
- The story success mindset invites you always to ask yourself: How does this story serve the room?
- By getting to know your audience model, you learn how to live in your audience's skin.
- Become aware of and limit your own biases that can short-circuit your success.

7. SIZZLING STARTS

'Where shall I begin?' asks the White Rabbit in Lewis Carroll's magical *Alice in Wonderland*. 'Begin at the beginning,' replies the King gravely, 'and go on till you come to the end: then stop.'

Beginnings in business storytelling are powerful moments. This is when your audience leans in and listens – or not.

> Your story beginning is the door to your audience's attention and heart. #StoryMastery

Story throat clearing squanders your audience's attention. A rambling beginning, too much context, false starts, telling your audience things they don't need to know or already know, beating around the bush:

> 'It was May 1984 ... no actually it was April, I remember now, it was close to my wedding anniversary and I never remember that date, which always gets me into trouble with my partner ...'

Yawn. The door to your audience's attention (and a warning: this door only ever opens a sliver) slams shuts. All the while giving the impression of being in the room with you (yes, all adults and particularly business professionals have mastered this art), your audience is probably thinking about what's for dinner tonight.

So many minefields await the unsuspecting storyteller. No wonder beginnings are often struggle street for leaders on their story mastery journey.

I have seen all of this happen again and again. There's a tension even before clients begin their stories. An awkwardness in the air, like a faltering conversation on a first date. Why all this awkwardness before we even start a story?

'Begin at the beginning' sounds like clear and succinct advice, yet it can still leave us floundering. Before we launch (begin) our story, we need to consider a segue sentence to ease us into the story naturally. Let me explain.

STORY SEGUES

Story segues are the velvet curtains that lead into the fortune-teller's tent – they part and lead your audience into your story. Segues make the difference between an awkward 'it's missing something' start or a smooth 'I want to hear more' start.

A story segue is a launchpad for your story. Former Police Commissioner of Victoria Christine Nixon was a master storyteller. She would often have to speak to dense PowerPoint slides in front of diverse audiences. She would read out a strategy point from the slide then step forward and say, 'For example, just yesterday I was talking to a farmer in Gippsland ...'

'For example' was her way of segueing into the beginning of the story. Neat, no?

Traffic will usually ease onto a busy freeway by means of a slip road. Think of your story segue as the slip road that allows you to move into your story safely.

Stories are like conversation dots. You can take a relevant story and insert it into a conversation, a meeting, a presentation, a pitch, but to do it successfully you need a segue sentence so your story is embedded naturally rather than jammed in arbitrarily.

Here are some examples of segues:

- I'd like to share a similar situation …
- I'm glad you mentioned that …
- I noticed on my way in …
- Can I look at the challenge another way? …
- That reminds me of when …
- What you said reminds me of …
- A time when I saw that working …
- Have you ever …
- To illustrate the point …
- Another way of looking at this …
- To explain what I mean …
- If you think that's funny you should hear this one! …
- I want to take a moment to share a relevant example …

Have you ever driven a manual car? Do you remember your first time? You start the engine, shift gears, slowly rolling off the clutch and the car jumps and jerks like a beast possessed. That's what starting a story without a segue can be for you and your audience.

Once you have your segue sentence, it's time to craft your beginning.

STORY BEGINNINGS

Recently at a storytelling masterclass a participant shared his story beginning. He delivered his line and stopped, which prompted a huge groan from around the room. Someone shouted out, 'We want to know what happened next!' That is exactly what a good, power-packed beginning can do for you.

I've already noted that in business a story should take between 30 seconds and two minutes to deliver. It's critical to remember that at this point, because beginnings are where many leaders fluff around and waste valuable time. To meet the tight timeframe a short, sharp beginning is key. Ideally, it should be one or at most two short sentences.

Here's an example of a story that hooks you in with a short sharp beginning.

STORY TITLE: THERAPY ANYONE?

One afternoon I was driving back from a visit to my therapist.

I had a vehement disagreement with her when she said I wasn't open to her ideas. The irony of the conversation, made me burst out laughing. Sometimes the things that are hardest to hear are the most important.

EMILY DEWBERRY, MEDIATOR, DEWBERRY MEDIATIONS PTY LTD

Here are some different ways to craft your beginning:

- Time and place
- Hook of surprise
- Provocative question
- Drop into emotion
- Dark start.

Let's look at each of these in detail.

Time and place

The classic way to begin a story in business (and this comes from the master himself, Steve Denning) is to register time and place. For example, 'When I was 10 we lived in St Kilda ...', or 'Yesterday at the gym', or 'In my last job with Qantas ...'

Time and place is a formula, but never formulaic, as there are infinite variations. Go to the time and place where this story begins and start there. In storytelling, small things make a big difference, and setting time and place in themselves signal that this is a story.

Never say, 'I'm going to tell you a story'. Amateur hour. Yikes! (More on mistakes people make with beginnings later in the chapter.) We use time and place to drop straight into the action. I cannot stress this enough.

In film schools across the world, students study the opening scene in Steven Spielberg's film *Saving Private Ryan*. In this harrowing, 30-minute battle scene we witness American soldiers storming Omaha Beach in Normandy on D Day. Spielberg drops us straight into the context of chaotic action. It's gruelling, gripping, and hooks us from the first frame.

For our own humble version of the start, using time and place should take us straight to the scene, to that moment in time, rather than getting caught up in too much detail.

It's also important to have a conversational energy around using time and place. Your beginning shouldn't sound like the start of a police report – 'At 5.45 pm, August 12th, in Melbourne CBD ...' – because no one talks like that, even on TV cop shows.

Avoid using both a date and another numeric like your age in the beginning. I have had clients say, for example, 'In 1998 when I was 21 ...' This excess information is likely to distract your audience, half of whom will be diverted into calculating the storyteller's age. I know, what can I say, we are easily distracted.

Used well, time and place works every time and is a safe place to start your story. It's worth exploring other possible beginnings, though, so you don't become too predictable.

Hook of surprise

Our brains love surprise. Research shows that the human brain is geared to notice the unusual. In an ocean of noise, something unexpected grabs our attention. Imagine this story beginning:

'Boxing promoter Don King was jailed for killing a man ...'

Some in the audience won't know that. Immediately their amygdala is leaning in, wanting to know what happened.

Remember this is business, so even a hint of something different throws a curve ball at your audience. It doesn't have to be a big Hollywood scene or a carefully orchestrated crime complete with a soundtrack.

For example, one of my stories starts with:

'Where were you on the 24th of June 1995?'

This gets the audience thinking and hooks them in.

Provocative question

'Have you ever hit rock bottom? I remember when I was 18 ...'

Questions at the start of a presentation or story are sadly underused. Yet the right question – for example, 'What stops us from reaching our potential?' – can capture your audience's imagination. The story that follows *must* link to and answer the question. That's important! If it fails in this, your audience's disappointment will cut deep.

I also like to raise the bar here. Why stop at just a question when you can build on that by asking a *provocative* question? In the sea of sanitised business communication, a provocative question can send a chill up your audience's spine, in a good way!

There is an art to nailing the right provocative question. Make it clean, crisp and economical. Like the example above: 'Have you ever hit rock bottom?' Six loaded words.

What matters is the storyteller's conviction. You've got to believe the question works for the story and be able to pull it off.

A micro-pause after the question is important. This gives your audience room to think and absorb it, and quantum leaps its impact. Sometimes repeating the question can also work. But always, always use a micro-pause after. No more than a couple of seconds, so no smart-arse has the chance to jump in with a response that disrupts the flow of your story.

In the pause, feel the energy of the question ripple through the audience like a Mexican wave. Ultimately, a provocative question heightens your audience's expectations. So the story that follows *must* deliver.

Drop into the emotion

'Manchester 2014. My heart was thumping …'

Please, what happens next? I *need* to know. Your audience crave answers. They are hungry for your story, burning with curiosity, their own adrenaline surging.

In storytelling, emotion at the start is like rocket fuel. Story blast-off guaranteed! It works best when the emotion you drop us straight into is what the key character is feeling. Even before you have delivered it, the audience invests in your story.

No click bait beginnings, please. You know, the ads that lure us in with a headline, promising so much then delivering dross. Any beginning, especially an emotive one, must deliver. Especially as the audience has heightened expectations.

Not every story lends itself to an emotive start. It might be hard to tap into much emotion when talking about an IT project, for example. *You* might love it and feel passionate, but your audience is unlikely to relate to your 'Be still my beating heart' start.

Emotive starts have to be relatable. In the story that follows, the audience must feel that, in your shoes, they would have felt the same way. Sorry to my IT friends.

Dark starts

'My name was Salmon, like the fish: first name Susie. I was fourteen when I was murdered on December 6, 1973.' This is how Alice Sebold's critically and commercially successful novel *The Lovely Bones* begins. That dark start pulls readers in from the first lines.

Business people often sugar-coat even the ugly stuff. A dark story start challenges norms and expectations. I am not mandating this kind of killer line for your beginning. Yet we can draw inspiration from many sources.

A dark start works well if there is an uplifting ending, or at least light at the end of the tunnel. This is not a business version of film noir. You don't want to follow a dark start with dark deeds and a devastating ending, leaving your audience depressed and despondent. Handcuff your inner Jean-Luc Godard, this is work!

One of my clients began with, 'Yesterday we received a customer complaint ...'

Yes, that's dark for business! He immediately had everyone's attention. He then talked about how one team member had stayed behind to work on the issue until she resolved it, and the glowing email they received from the customer.

A dark start must be followed by an upward trajectory. Finish the story on a high. The contrast should be strong. Take your audience from a dark place and leave them dazzled by the light of hope and optimism.

Spend time writing up your story beginning. You could use any of the beginnings we have suggested. Or at this point, keep it simple and just use time and place.

COCO CHANEL

Do you remember Coco Chanel's famous advice? 'Always remove one accessory before leaving the house. Less is more.' You have your start down (one sentence, or two short ones) – now 'Coco Chanel' it by taking something out.

When we first meet Hannibal Lecter (Anthony Hopkins) in *The Silence of the Lambs* he is just standing calmly, arms by his sides, his body and face at rest, expressionless. He doesn't say anything. Yet it is *so* chilling. It's the perfect introduction to the character and a wonderful example of less is more.

No one, not even Stephen King, can write a perfect beginning sentence in one hit, so you are in good company. Only by drafting and redrafting the beginning can we get it right and give the rest of our story the best chance of success.

The simplest and most effective way to do that is to trim it back, pare it down, Coco Chanel it. The rest of your story can be pure Versace, but for your beginning, I insist you channel Coco.

Compare these two beginnings before and after Coco.

Pre-Coco:

'I've been through many difficulties in my life and I have learned that what matters is that it is other people who love you who can get you through it. When I was 19 I lost my mother to cancer.'

Post-Coco:

'When I was 19, I lost my mother to cancer.'

It's the second version that packs a punch, landing the audience straight in the emotion. It is easy to Coco Chanel your beginnings. It requires only that you be detached and objective. Take out a few words, trim it back and see if it works.

I also recommend saying your beginning aloud. It gives you a sense of what works orally. Stripping back your beginning is what story masters do.

> Coco Chaneling your beginning turns all your beginning pumpkins into carriages. Guaranteed. #StoryMastery

MISTAKES WITH BEGINNINGS

There are as many ways *not* to begin your story. The wrong beginning will give a story cardiac arrest. A bad beginning slays the story that follows.

Fairy stories traditionally start with the words 'Once upon a time'. Avoid this beginning at all costs unless your audience is made up of preschoolers.

Using an opener such as 'Let me tell you a story' isn't much better. Do you ever begin a data presentation with 'Let me tell you a statement of fact'? The idea is ridiculous. Just the same, in storytelling 'Let me tell you a story' is a redundant beginning.

Using such wording can detract from the seriousness of your message and can sound patronising. It does your story a disservice, robbing what follows of its potency.

Even worse is to make the claim that what follows is 'a true story', because listeners will immediately conclude that it's not!

Detailed context is a poor place to start too. You might deem that some background is important to the story, but if you cannot express what is important in one or two sentences, then my advice is not to use this story. It won't work, because you'll lose people in this densely forested context.

Giving away the ending at the start also doesn't serve your story well. This is a common mistake. It's like opening a thriller to find someone has scrawled the name of the murderer on the first page.

You would want to murder *them* if you could only find them. Or is that just me?

When we know how it will end, or what it's about, we tend to lose interest. Leaders often give away too much too soon. 'I want to share a time when I discovered the importance of teamwork.' Save this for your ending.

Telling the audience what your story is about risks dumbing it down. It can sound as though your audience has to have things spelled out or they won't get it. Of course not all of your audience will be as perceptive or sensitive to slight, but such a beginning can work against you.

Sometimes presenters will begin with a disclaimer. Even one as simple as 'To cut a long story short' makes you sound lazy as a storyteller and is annoying for your audience, who wonder what they missed out on and how long this will take. It makes you sound amateurish, as though you haven't prepared properly.

Often we use expressions like this as 'brain burps'. We say them out of habit or because we are nervous, but they gross an audience out.

By practising the techniques, and avoiding the pitfalls, outlined in this chapter, you are well on your way to nailing your beginnings. Next we'll look at how to make your story middles sing.

KEY INSIGHTS

- A good story beginning holds the key to your story success.
- Stories need to be introduced by a segue sentence before you even use your beginning. Segues let you ease into your story and avoid an awkward or abrupt start.
- Once you have your segue, choose a beginning form – from the humble 'time and place' to the rigours of the 'dark start'.
- Your story beginning should be no more than one or two sentences, and should be pared back for maximum impact.
- Avoid amateur mistakes with your beginnings, such as 'Let me tell you a story' or revealing your ending.
- Once you have written your beginning down, say it aloud. Does it work orally?
- Play with your beginnings, have fun and own them. Then so will your audience.

8. THE MAGIC OF MIDDLES

Story middles are sometimes treated like middle children. At some stage we have all bought into the 'neglected middle child' cliché (with apologies to my elder sister). First-borns are assigned the greatest responsibility, while the last-borns are indulged as charming and rebellious. As a last-born, I concur!

However, in a recent book titled *The Secret Power of Middle Children*, Catherine Salmon and Katrin Schumann argue that middle children often turn this neglect into a huge positive advantage. Many turn out to be good mediators and diplomats; 52 per cent of American presidents have been middle children.

Compared with story beginnings and endings, story middles tend to be marginalised. I describe story beginnings and endings as power moments. Story beginnings are the decisive point when you persuade your audience to lean in. Endings are powerful too, when your audience 'gets it', the *aha* moment that inspires them or propels them into action. The right ending lands your story.

> Beginnings target your audience's attention, middles transport your audience to a different time and place and endings transform your audience #StoryMastery

Middles let most stories down. Recently I took part in a Melbourne Moth StorySLAM. (You can check out my video online and I link to it at the back of the book.) Yes, I won. No, there was no unfair advantage, as the rules are so different. (Imagine having to make excuses for winning!)

At The Moth, they keep score on a whiteboard, so everyone knows the tally. I was the front-runner, then there was one storyteller who was brilliant. Brilliant. My heart sank to my feet (well I'm only human). I was sure she'd win, knocking me off my perch. And then she had one line, just one line, in her middle that left the audience cold. She snatched defeat from the jaws of victory.

I like to pretend magnanimously that I was gutted for her. Closer to the truth would be I was relieved for myself! I had kept my first place and felt the chill of that close call. I congratulated her and told her I loved her story and felt it would be a perfect TED talk (yes I am a good person, thank you).

But what the experience taught me is how potent middles can be. The middle is the magic that connects your beginning and your ending. It gives your story momentum and action and keeps your audience invested.

Dan Gregory is an expert in influence and leadership, and a regular on ABC TV's *Gruen* and the Seven Network's *Sunrise*. Gregory reckons fame opens doors for him, but then he has to have *game*. This is just how I see story beginnings and middles. Beginnings are like fame. If your beginning is good, it will open the door, capturing your audience's attention, but then you have to have game. Your middle has to keep this attention going. So GAME ON with your middle!

WHAT IS THE PURPOSE OF A MIDDLE?

Once you have set the stage with your punchy beginning, you have our attention. Hopefully, your beginning was so good we are all dying to know what happens next. Now your middle, where the plot unfolds, has to work hard to sustain our attention.

In the example below, we break a story into its component parts and look closely at the middle to see what makes it tick.

STORY TITLE: DON'T SWEAT THE SMALL STUFF

Beginning: It was January 2005, a hot stinky summer's day in Melbourne, and the trains were running late.

Middle: Finally a city loop train appeared and I squeezed on, knowing if I missed it I'd be late to work. The train was packed. I could barely breathe. Every time the train stopped more people tried to squeeze in. It was unbearably hot and I was wedged under someone's armpit. Everyone was moaning and groaning. I stood there, looking around, and reflected on what had happened only a few weeks ago, when the Boxing Day tsunami had struck Thailand, leaving thousands of people's lives in ruin. So many children lost parents, families ripped apart. And here we were complaining about an overcrowded train.

Ending: I instantly felt myself relax as my mindset shifted that day. *Don't sweat the small stuff.*

STORYTELLER: LEANNE MICALLEF, TAC

HOW TO CREATE MAGIC MIDDLES

The middle is the chunkiest section of the story. It's where we spend the most time both when we are drafting it and when we are sharing it.

The following techniques can make our story middles potent.

Fly on the wall

In the first 10 minutes of *The Matrix*, you see Trinity take out five cops effortlessly. Then an Agent shows up, and she runs. Within the first 10 minutes of the movie, you know Trinity is a badass and you're already scared of the antagonists. At no point is there a voice-over narration saying watch out for Trinity, she's a badass. It is like we are flies on the wall, watching the action explode.

While we don't have Hollywood's big budget and sensational special effects, we can borrow what they do. The best movies let us experience the action, as if we are a fly on the wall. We watch the action as it unfolds.

In the 'Don't sweat the small stuff' story above, with every word storyteller Leanne Micallef puts us in the frame. It is as if we are living the crowded train experience with her. That is what your middle should do for your audience. They should experience the story as if they are a fly on the wall – they are totally immersed in the action as it unfolds.

Imagine a middle where we say 'Jane was angry'. This is ho-hum. Compare that with 'Jane slammed her fists on the table'. The second version immerses your audience in the action – they feel Jane's emotion.

As you are sharing what happens next in your story, always check you're showing your audience the action, not telling them what to think. The question to ask is, 'If my audience were a fly on the wall what would they see next?' And describe that.

I recently heard someone describe their experience in Thailand during the tsunami of 2004. They started off strongly, saying, 'I remembered waking up in Thailand on Boxing Day 2004 to the news that a tsunami had struck'. Then they said, 'That day I saw the best of humanity, the worst of humanity. I saw how people came together in adversity. I saw strangers become family. I saw grief and hope.'

Awww, the missed opportunity of this story made me want to weep. If instead the storyteller thought of the fly on the wall technique for their middle, they would have shown us what happened next. A stranger giving his last bottle of water to a child. A mother who had lost her own children in the waves immediately taking charge of and comforting two orphans.

When you show the audience (using the fly on the wall technique), they feel the emotion. They are immersed in the action.

Coffee with a friend

Even though we write our stories down, it's very important to keep the tone conversational. Good stories have a 'coffee with a friend' energy about them. If you were describing what happened next to a friend, what would you say?

Coffee with a friend energy keeps our stories real – it's the sound of one human being talking to another. This energy also keeps our stories intimate. A great story should always feel like you're talking to just one other person, irrespective of the scale of the story itself. So whether you are sharing your story with one other person or a hundred, this conversational tone will keep your story intimate. In the delivery section we will talk more extensively about scale, but it all pivots on intimacy. The intimacy that you create through being conversational with your stories.

You would never say, 'I met Bill to discuss how we might optimise synergies.' Eww! No one talks to their friends like that. Or if you do then, ahem, I'm surprised you have any friends left! You would probably say something like, 'So I met Bill and I asked him what was getting in the way of our working together.'

The other rule to follow here is to keep your story absolutely jargon free. Jargon creep usually happens in the middle. We are jargon vigilant in our starts and, usually, our ends because we recognise that beginnings and endings are story power moments. But we tend to be rather more relaxed in the middle of the story.

Jargon is nuclear radiation for stories. Think of this graphic metaphor whenever you are seduced to put even the tiniest bit of jargon into your story. It will destroy your whole story. I'm not being dramatic, just brutally honest, but it is confronting because it challenges us to rethink and recast familiar, conventional jargon into more human language.

But don't worry, you don't have to struggle with this alone. There are handy apps and websites that help you do this. The site Unsuck It, for example, has the tagline 'What terrible business jargon do you need unsucked?' and is a good pit stop, as is Business Jargon Translator, with its tagline 'Make your message authentic and human'.

Sensory detail

Angry red face, squeaky high-pitched voice, deep golden sunset. Did your mind immediately conjure up images (or sounds) for each of these phrases? When storytellers appeal to any of our five senses – sight, sound, touch, smell or taste – they are weaving in sensory detail. Rich sensory detail makes stories come alive. So much of the blandness in business-speak comes from lack of sensory texture. Sensory detail can make your middle pop.

Why is this so important? When you picture a scene in your mind you are using the same visual cortex as when you see something through your eyes. So when you describe walking down a dark path in the forest, your audience can see this, as though they were there with you. Marketer and business writer Ann Handley says, 'Words are evocative. They're visceral. They're nuanced and complicated. Words are power travelers who packed lots of emotion and baggage – freight that doesn't easily fit in an overhead bin space.'

Here are some questions to ask yourself when drafting your middle that will help you find evocative sensory detail:

- What do I want my audience to see? (a golden sunset)
- What do I want them to hear? (the sound of waves crashing)
- What do I want them to touch? (silky as a new-born kitten)
- What do I want them to smell? (like a fish market)
- What do I want them to taste (a hot beer on a cold day)

A rule of thumb is to use only one or two sensory details, or you risk overloading both your story and your audience and losing your main message.

The exception to this rule is when, as in the 'Don't sweat the small stuff' story, sensory detail builds up the atmosphere. You raise the stakes and then – *wham* – you contrast it with the human catastrophe of the tsunami. Here the sensory detail serves a clear purpose, and the story remains tight.

Middling length

The middle section of your story is the longest to tell and to draft. It follows your short, punchy beginning and precedes (as we will see) a brief starburst ending.

If your story takes two minutes to tell, spend up to 30 seconds on your beginning and up to 30 seconds on your ending, dedicating at least half your time to the middle. Again, this is a rule of thumb only; no one will be holding a stopwatch and timing you.

The middle is where the action unfolds. As the longest part, it's also the danger zone, where your audience's attention is most likely to sag. To sustain their attention use all the techniques discussed in this chapter:

- 'Fly on the wall' draws your audience straight into the action.
- Coffee with a friend keeps the story intimate, with each member of your audience feeling you are speaking just to them.
- Sensory detail engages your audience's senses, grabbing their attention and immersing them in the story.

These three techniques make the difference between a middling middle and a magic middle.

In the next chapter we will look at how to end our story, so it packs a punch.

KEY INSIGHTS

- Middles can be a story minefield or a magical link between your beginning and ending.
- Don't underestimate their power to make or break a story.
- The fly on the wall technique lets your audience experience the story directly.
- Coffee with a friend energy keeps your stories real – one human being talking to another.
- When storytellers appeal to any of our five senses – sight, sound, touch, smell or taste – they are weaving in sensory detail.
- Sensory detail makes your middles pop.
- These techniques help craft a compelling middle that holds your audience riveted, invested and yearning for more.

9. POWER ENDINGS

'After all, tomorrow is another day,' Southern belle Scarlett O'Hara says at the end of the bestseller *Gone with the Wind*. Everyone remembers or knows that famous last line. It brims with potential and leaves the audience wanting more, even though the novel is 1,037 pages long! Author Margaret Mitchell understood the power of a good ending.

Storytelling in a novel is like swimming in the ocean – you have all the 'time and place' in the world. Business storytelling, though, is like swimming in a bathtub. It has to be short and tight, with a sharp, concise ending of no more than a line or two.

An ending leaves your audience with a message without banging them over the head with it. You imply, suggest or invite but never dictate what your audience should get from your story. 'Invitation is the soul of the work,' says Dr Betty Sargeant, a multi-award winning Australian artist and designer.

That is what we are aiming for with our endings.

In the table below, we can see the impact different endings has on an audience and also their perception of you as a storyteller. Everything we work on next will help us create power endings to leave our audience feeling inspired.

FIGURE 9.1: IMPACT OF DIFFERENT ENDINGS

STORYTELLER STATUS	ENDING TYPE	AUDIENCE REACTION
Legend/Master	Power ending	Inspired
Safe	Predictable	Bored
Controlling	Forced	Backlash
Conservative	Cliched	Disappointed
Amateur	No ending	Confused

ENDING ANGST

Endings are powerful moments in storytelling. The right ending lands your story and turns an average story into a blockbuster.

To make sure this happens I encourage my clients to be prepared to suffer some ending angst. I know this sounds like a first-world problem. Even Hollywood endings can cause sleepless nights. Recognising their importance, studios will often audience test different endings to help them nail it.

Call me a story tyrant, but I recommend this level of testing at a minimum, and let's even throw in some insomnia in our quest for the right ending.

Why this level of angst? Because the ending will make or break a story; it can turn a crowd against you, or leave an audience misty-eyed or flood them with hope. Ending, thou art KING! Sorry, got carried away there.

So you need to work on your ending. It's the last thing your audience hears, and the recency factor will ensure it's what they will remember – today, tomorrow and into the future. No pressure, though!

One of my clients has a story superpower. He's a natural at crafting the perfect ending. It became such a running joke that we affectionately called him 'Punchline Paul'. This chapter shows you how to make story endings your superpower too – with apologies to Paul!

WHERE TO START WITH YOUR ENDINGS?

To unpack your ending, first ask yourself a simple question:

'What is the message I want to leave my audience with?'

or

'What is the point of this story?'

In business storytelling, the message or point *becomes* your ending. So before creating your ending you must be clear on the message. Otherwise it is like building a bridge without knowing where it is you want to end up.

Don't worry if the point of your story is not a 100 per cent clear as yet. It could be something as loose as 'I want my team to share information' or 'I want people to step up into challenges'. Right now you need coal. Once you have it, I'll show you how to polish it into an ending diamond.

Spend a minute or two writing up or thinking about your message or point.

WAYS TO END

There are many ways you can end your story. Like hats, you have to try on a few to find what fits best – for you, your story and your audience.

Don't settle for the first ending that comes to mind. This is the one time I advocate promiscuity. Comedians learn quickly that the first funny thing that jumps into their mind in any context (airline food, fast cars, late nights) will probably have occurred to others too. So you write as many variations on the joke as you can before arriving at the best one, which is rarely the first one that struck you.

Ending monogamy takes time, trial and error, and patience. Here are some ways to write your ending. Read the whole list and try out a few to see what works best for the story you have in mind.

Bridge and link

A business story, particularly a lateral business story (which we cover in chapter 4), merits a two-part ending. The first part (perhaps the first sentence) is a bridge that brings people back into the room, back into the work context. The second part (or sentence) links to the message or point of the story. This idea of a bridge and link ending comes from Stephen Denning, the founder of the field of business storytelling.

Let's look at the bridge and link ending in the apple story from the introduction:

My little five-year-old niece Maya walked into the house yesterday, holding a ripe apple in each hand. I thought this would be the perfect time to role model sharing! I asked her, 'Maya, can I please have an apple?' She looked at me and immediately bit into the apple in her right hand. Then just as quickly she took a bite out of the apple in her left hand. I was shocked. But before I could react she held out the apple in her left hand, saying, 'Here aunty, take this one – it's sweeter'.

The ending:

I'm sharing this because so often we jump to conclusions about people's behaviour. Imagine if sometimes we took a step back and paused.

The bridge:

I'm sharing this because so often we jump to conclusions about people's behaviour.

Helps your audience come back into the room and also pre-empts the response, 'What does this have to do with us at work?' It's also a bridge to your last line.

The link:

Imagine if sometimes we took a step back and paused.

Links to the point you are making. Notice the point is not hammered home; rather, it is subtly suggested.

Contrast this with:

I am telling you this. Because what I want you to do is to take a step back and pause.

The *I am telling you this ...* bridge and link fall short on three counts:

- *I am telling you this* is instructive, hierarchical. Replace this with *I'm sharing this*, which is conversational and inclusive.
- *What I want you to do* is didactic and can turn your audience off. Substitute with *Imagine if*, which is an invitation.
- The pronoun *you* makes this sound like a command. Use the pronoun *we* for inclusive potency.

Here are suggestions for bridging sentences:

- *That experience reminds me of what we are trying to achieve here.*
- *That mattered because today we are in a similar situation.*
- *I thought of that because our context is so similar.*

You could also be provocative with your bridge and ask, 'So what does this have to do with work?' Usually a conversational bridge works best. Express it in the language you would normally use in conversation.

For your linking sentence, the challenge is to couch it as an invitation and inspiration. Storytelling is about moving from 'command and control' to 'engage and enrol'. Your linking sentence should engage your audience and enlist them in your purpose. Here are a few suggestions to get you going:

- *Imagine if ...*

- *The difference we could make ...*
- *Just let's think about ...*

Zing words

Some endings have a word that zings, that pops. Zing words are the most positive words in the ending. Moving zing words, so they are the last words you say quantum leaps the impact of your story.

Finding and ending on zing words is a well-used comedic device. Groucho Marx said, 'Outside of a dog, a book is a man's best friend. Inside of a dog, it's too dark to read'. He ends on the zing words – 'too dark to read'.

It would not be so funny if he'd said: 'It's too dark to read inside a dog'. Ending on zing words is a trick we should borrow as storytellers.

Not every ending has zing words in it that can be conveniently relocated to finish on. Also, be careful not to sound like Yoda from *Star Wars* in your pursuit of a zing finish! It can seem contrived and you might have people laughing at you, rather than with you.

Here's an example to convey the power of zing words.

Compare these two endings:

- *That day I got the gift of feedback.*
- *That day I saw feedback as a gift.*

Two crucial words here: *gift* and *feedback*. Gift, a zing word, is more potent than feedback. It also helps you end your story on a positive note, rather than the negativity sometimes associated with the word feedback, which comes with more baggage than gift. Not my rules, but how most people would feel. Just saying!

Sometimes you don't have just zing words, but a potential zing sentence! To explain a zing sentence makes you more likable as a storyteller and leaves your audience in a better space.

Compare these two endings:

- *I now run four times a week.*
- *Running is now part of my life.*

The first ending might leave your audience thinking, good on you but that's not for me. Even if unintentional, it suggests a certain smugness (wrapped in achievement). This is off-putting for an audience. The tough news is audiences can turn on a dime. They can love you and your story all the way through and then – BANG – an un-empathic ending like that can throw them offside completely.

The second ending has more zing! It's more likable and leaves your audience in a different space. It makes them think about things (maybe running, maybe quite different) that have become part of their life. We've all been there. It's inclusive so bound to be a winner.

Natural finish

In a handful of stories, the message is so self-evident that you need not think, design and test an ending. In a natural finish the story carries the learning within it, like a baby kangaroo hidden in its mother's pouch. There is no need for you to add another ending and mess with perfection.

A natural finish doesn't require your story to have a message tacked onto its end. #StoryMastery

Tacking on an ending diminishes the story. This is a relatively new learning for me and I am still coming to terms with it. Initially aiming for a natural finish felt like skydiving with a parachute you bought at a car boot sale. Scary and death-defying.

So what makes it worth it? A natural finish (in business where everything is firmly nailed down) can be a thing of beauty and joy. And it's deeply respectful of your audience. It says, I know you are intelligent and will get this. I won't dumb it down and labour the point.

In my decade of practice as a storyteller, I have encountered only one or two natural finishes that worked! Here is an example. The audience responded with three 'Awws' when they heard it the first time.

STORY TITLE: WHAT'S LOVE GOT TO DO WITH IT?

When I was young, we would go every Saturday to my granny's house for lunch. There were about twenty of us and Granny would cook up a huge meal. She was so caring and would cater for everyone's needs.

I had a cousin who hated peas in his potato salad, so she would make a dish just for him with potato salad without peas. Another cousin didn't like passionfruit pips in sponge cake icing, so she would get a special slice of cake without passionfruit pips in the icing, while the rest of us got the normal passionfruit sponge cake. My aunty loved cashews and Granny found the most economical way to get them was to buy mixed nuts and carefully pick out the cashews for her.

I once told her, 'Don't go to all this trouble, it's so much work. Just make one meal and we can all make do'. Granny put her arm around me and said, 'This is something I can afford to do for my family'.

STORYTELLER: CHLOE MCDOUGALL, AIA AUSTRALIA

You could tack on an ending to this – for example, *When we love people it's not work* – but the story is beautiful as it is. The audience can take so much from this story without having a message spelt out.

A natural finish is the unicorn of business storytelling. It's totally worth pursuing, but we must acknowledge that it is a rare and magical beast.

Sometimes, though, you probably will stumble on a natural finish. You are sharing your story and you feel your audience get it. You just sense it. You viscerally know you don't need to tie it up neatly with a bow, because this is the perfect end point for the story.

As much as it might tempt you, don't use your ambition for a natural finish to cop out of the work of carefully crafting an ending. If you use a natural finish when the story is not yet resolved, it will leave your audience puzzled and confused. And for you as storyteller it is a lost opportunity. In this case, not using a tailored ending will probably mean your story won't land.

THE ENERGY OF ENDINGS

Storytelling is experiential – you experience it and feel it and can't always explain every element. Have you ever met someone and just hit it off straight away, yet you can't put your finger on exactly what made you click? Or walked into a place and immediately walked out again, because something about the vibe put you off? Story endings, too, have a vibe about them, an energy that your audience senses. Just as story beginnings carry the energy of a promise or a hook, endings also have a certain energy about them.

Endings work best when the energy is inclusive and is an invitation.

> Inclusive + Invitation = Inspiration #StoryMastery

How do we get this kind of energy into our endings? Small words can make a big difference.

Sharing not telling

Always choose 'sharing' over 'telling'. Sharing is inclusive (think the new sharing economy), telling is old school (think coal mines and the industrial era).

Using we

With endings, 'we' works better than 'you'. The inclusive *we* signals that all of us are in this together. The use of the word 'we' is a great leveller. It positions the storyteller and story listener as equals.

Invitation

The ending should always invite your audience into a brighter future or a new possibility. And perversely this seems to work best when you *don't* use the word invitation. Think of it as playing charades where you can't use the word you want people to guess.

I won't say you cannot use the word invite; sometimes it might work, but most times we want the 'vibe' of the word without its direct use.

Consider this example:

> I'm sharing this because it reminded me so much of what we do at work every day. Imagine the difference we could make if we saw every customer that way.

Even though the storyteller was the boss, he used the inclusive we, ending with an invitation. An invitation to make a difference through our customer interactions. A promise of a brighter world. I had goose bumps when I heard this the first time. Me, a seasoned storyteller. Imagine the impact it had on the audience.

If you're feeling particularly curmudgeonly, you might argue that this ending could have worked as well with the word invitation in it. I will not fence with you on this point! But I do suggest that a story master would steer clear of the word or at least use it sparingly.

Using the words *sharing* and *we* and the energy of an invitation in your ending also ensures that you as storyteller don't sound like you're blaming others (the audience) or making demands of them that you are not making of yourself.

Storytelling is a great leveller. It subtly dismantles hierarchy. It centres us on what connects us – our humanity. Gentle words like 'sharing' and 'we' do the heavy lifting.

It's the vibe

Over two decades ago the iconic Australian film *The Castle* burst onto our screens. Even today, so many years later, some lines remain popular. One of my favourites is when the lawyer pleading his client's case to keep his home argues, 'It's the vibe and … ah … no that's it. It's the vibe. I rest my case.'

I too rest my case for the energy of the right endings. Following my own advice, I'm sharing this with you, because with the right energy imagine the difference we could make with our story endings.

ENDINGS DO'S AND DON'TS

The best do for an ending is to have one! Highly recommend – 5 stars, standing ovation, you get the gist. And no, it can't be 'The End' or 'That's all, folks'. The only exception to this rule is, as explained above, if you have found a natural finish to your story and it doesn't need to be tied up with a bow.

Endings should always be positive. Check out these two examples.

Ending 1
That day, my life was in shreds, leaving me anxious about my future.

Ending 2
That day, my life was in shreds, leaving me anxious about my future. [Pause] I decided it was time for me to step up.

The first ending leaves your audience in a dark place. They feel bad for you but are not sure what to do next. You want to maintain the honesty and authenticity of this ending, yet you also want to leave the audience with some hope. So you add the second sentence (which is also true). You can hear the audience sigh in relief. Your audience now knows you are okay, that you're on your way back up, and that makes them feel good too.

As storyteller, you get to choose where to end, so aim for a positive, uplifting finish. Steve Denning says fairy tales always end with 'And they lived happily ever after'. 'No one wants to know that the princess suffered from an eating disorder and could look forward to divorce and a sadly early death.' Yes, call it shallow, but life is hard enough without adding sad endings to your business stories.

Multiple endings

My pet peeve here is multiple endings, where the storyteller aims for a big bang finish by packing everything in. If you try this, instead of a bang you'll end up bombing.

For example:

> 'I'm sharing this with you because it reminds me of the opportunity we have every day to role model courage, innovation, customer service, standing up for yourself and challenging the status quo.'

Whoa! Hello! You lost your audience at courage.

In Melbourne, where we love and live for our coffee, we also know any coffee order cannot have more than three words in it. Otherwise, you are in grave danger of tripping over into princess territory. My current drink of choice is a soy chai latte (can't be strong or skinny or have anything else added to it). I've already maxed out.

I'm even more restrictive about story endings. Only one ending. If my coffee order was a story ending, I would have to choose either soy or chai or latte. So tough – no, please spare me. But this is the same hard prioritising you are going to have to make for your story ending. Decide up front on your ending, rather than overwhelming your audience by throwing in everything and hoping for the best.

What makes this hard is that most stories are rich and layered, and you feel like you're compromising by landing your story on just one thing, like they have clipped your wings.

You are thinking Google Earth – big, impressive scale – and I'm saying zoom, zoom, zoom in, from city to suburb to street to house, for your ending. Trust me, your audience will take away much more than what you actually say in the ending. Your job at this point is to trust them and focus them on one point and one point only.

You want your audience to drink from a glass of water, not from a fire hydrant. Which is what multiple endings feel like. They leave your audience drenched, overwhelmed and – this is the tragedy – still thirsty.

Rambling

The other ending 'don't' is the rambling ending, where the storyteller unpacks the whole story again and explains exactly what they meant. In comedy, the equivalent is explaining a joke down to joke structure, construction and delivery. Very unfunny and tedious.

A rambling explanatory ending is grossly insulting for your audience, not to say patronising, offensive and boring. They have arrested people for less. It's also lazy storytelling. It looks like the storyteller isn't prepared and is doing this on the fly. Or they are talking only for the sake of hearing their own voice.

Sharing a story is like filling a balloon with helium, full of hope, ready to fly. A rambling ending lets all the helium out, deflating the story and your audience.

Evangelical endings

But wait, I'm saving the worst for last. This is more than a peeve – this kind of ending needs its own protest march, with banners and merchandise, a petition to Parliament to change law.

It is the evangelical ending. The storyteller gets on their moral high horse and tells the audience to do the same. To take the high road as they have done. Sometimes feeling this is not enough, they must also shame the audience for their current practices. Shame and blame. Way to go – NOT! Yes, I'm shouting.

Consider:

> 'That day I changed my water usage habits. Shame on everyone who thinks this is too hard. I could do it, my family could do it. What are you waiting for? Another drought? We all have to do the right thing, as I did.'

Some endings polarise an audience, some leave them shell-shocked. An ending like this means the audience will leave no stone unturned, and they'll hurl every one of them at the storyteller.

Okay, I exaggerated that, but I want to spell out this point. The storyteller should never place themselves on a pedestal. There can be no judgement or superiority in your ending.

A WORD TO THE WISE

A well-known concept in economics is the law of diminishing returns. In simple terms, it tells us that after a certain point the more you put into something the less you get back.

The idea has broader applications outside of economics. Think of how good that first piece of cake tastes, then the second piece not so good, and the third – yuck! Diminishing returns in action. In a call centre, service-level improvements decline in proportion to each additional agent employed. So what does this have to do with endings in story-telling? Storytelling, like most things in life, is subject to this law.

Do you remember the famous line in the film *Jerry Maguire*, when Jerry (Tom Cruise) flies back home to meet Dorothy (Renée Zellweger) to tell her, far too circuitously, that he loves her? She stops him: 'Shut up. Just shut up! You had me at hello.' Our challenge is to find that same 'sweet spot' in our story where we have our audience – and to stop the story right there.

For storytellers that sweet spot is when you end at the exact moment when you have your audience, because if your story continues beyond this point you'll lose them, as the law of diminishing returns kicks in.

End your story at the top of the curve, with your audience wanting more. Just like cake, know when to stop.

In the next chapter we will learn how to put our beginning, middle and ending together so we have a complete story that flows.

KEY INSIGHTS

- The right ending lands your story and turns an average story into a blockbuster.
- In business storytelling, the message or point *becomes* your ending.
- A business story can have a two-part ending: the first part is a bridge that brings people back into the work context; the second part links to the message or point of the story.
- Zing words are the most potent words in the ending; moving them so they are the last words quantum leaps story impact.
- Some stories have a natural finish and don't need a message tacked on.
- Endings work best when the energy is inclusive and inviting.
- Aim for positive endings; avoid multiple, rambling or evangelical endings.

10. PUTTING IT ALL TOGETHER

You have done the hard work and produced a piecemeal version of your story – crafted your beginning, your middle and your ending. The next step is to pull it all together – and you have your first completed story.

Once you have done so, you need to check a few things, to step back from the story and make sure it all works. Is the whole greater than the sum of its parts? What adjustments are needed? Specifically, check:

- flow
- form
- finesse.

Let's explore each of these elements in detail.

FLOW

Flow carries your audience through the story with you. To check for flow, ask yourself some tough questions:

- Do the three parts of the story work together seamlessly?
- Does it make logical sense?

There should be no gaps in the logic. Your audience should not need to make any big leaps. Is each part of the story credible? We had a client start a story with 'At the 2000 Athens Olympics'. We had to stop it right there. If there's one date that's imprinted in the memory of all Australian sports lovers it's 2000, when Sydney hosted the Olympics. Such an error would derail your entire story.

Check you are not making assumptions about your audience's knowledge. Storytelling works best when we tap into existing schemas in our audience's heads. Existing schemas are common experiences or knowledge we share on how the world works. For example, stories about watching the evening news, waiting in an airport security queue or attending your child's parent–teacher interview need no additional knowledge on your audience's part. These stories leverage existing schemas.

What if your story is about a schema that your audience may not already have in their head? One of my clients is a self-confessed science nerd. He shared a story about the 2017 Saturn landing. For him this was huge, huge news and very exciting. To his dismay, he quickly picked up from the audience's body language their lack of both knowledge and interest. Someone said to him, 'Oh, that didn't come up on my Facebook feed'.

When you share a story that doesn't tap into existing schemas, you are engaging with what I call story outliers.

Story outliers

In statistics, an outlier is an observation that is far removed from the others in the data set and can cause serious problems in statistical analysis.

In his bestseller *Outliers: The Story of Success*, Malcolm Gladwell defines outliers as people who do not fit into our normal understanding of achievement and operate at the extreme outer edge of what is statistically plausible. The book focuses on exceptional people, especially those who are smart, rich and successful (Bill Gates, The Beatles), and the factors that contribute to high levels of success.

The problem with using a story outlier is that you risk making your audience feel dumb and putting them offside, causing them to stop listening and disengage. That's the bad news. But wait, there's good news too!

I still urge you to use your story outliers (which could be your hobbies or passions outside of work), no matter how niche (vintage washing machines from the 1960s anyone?). Why persist in the face of such challenges? Isn't it safer to stick with well-worn stories?

Audiences are oh so bored

A lot of seasoned leaders tell me they can't hack one more story about Steve Jobs or Richard Branson. We have done these stories to death, so audiences are as hungry for something different as zombies for fresh meat (thumbs up for all the zombie genre fans out there). Audiences crave novelty. If you don't get that metaphor, just go with the idea, thanks.

Australia's most popular TV quiz show understands this. *Hard Quiz* is the name of the show. The participants are experts in one narrow niche area, like origami or the movie versions of Jane Austen's *Pride and Prejudice*, or an obscure historical figure. They are total nerds in this one area of expertise and are quizzed on their niche area and other general knowledge questions. The show is chart-bustlingly popular because you never know what you'll get. Even the quiz master has confessed the challenge of coming up with questions sometimes. This format makes for amusing and interesting viewing. *Hard Quiz* has found juju and discovered a winner in shaking up the tired old TV quiz format.

When you light up over your niche expertise or interest, your audience can feel it. It gives your story a hum, an energy, that is priceless. Your enthusiasm, authenticity and passion are the fuel for this kind of story.

Raising the bar

There is a second reason to stick with your story outliers. I never want to deter you from raising the intellectual bar for any audience! We can dumb down our audience or their expectations sometimes. This kind of story says you respect both your audience's intellect and their ability to learn. Set yourself up for success by telling stories that are elegant and inclusive, and you can turn the outlier barrier into a huge advantage.

Social capital

Audiences love 'dinner-table fodder', something they can take away and use to impress their friends with at their next dinner party. Story outliers are great for creating this 'social capital'. So how do you turn your audiences on, rather than off? One way is to be self-deprecating. You need to give your audience just enough context so they understand the story, but without patronising them. For my client's story, I suggested the following beginning:

'I'm a total science nerd. Since 1997 I've been following NASA's spacecraft *Cassini*. I know, two decades – I'm like a space stalker. So imagine my sadness when on September 15 last year *Cassini* made its final approach to Saturn. But this encounter was like no other ... '

That was enough context and a solid hook to get the audience engaged without feeling stupid. By admitting you're a science nerd, you let everyone else off the hook. You don't expect them to know about *Cassini* because they aren't nerds. Glancing around the room they see lots of people like them, and that makes it okay. Now they can sit back and enjoy the story, because they have the context. Of course, they can also earn kudos for this nugget when they casually weave it into that next dinner-party conversation. And believe me, a lot of them will!

Checking for flow ensures you turn on the tap of your audience's attention so they stay with you all the way through the story.

This is also the point to check that your story doesn't cast you in a heroic light while throwing shade over everyone else! Your audience may not respond to this positively. Sometimes might be okay – for example, when you faced down to the school bully – but if all your stories follow this formula, you will become less likable and therefore less successful as a storyteller. Variety is king. Sometimes you can be the hero (it's your life, so your story), but I strongly recommend sharing the spotlight. When you make someone else the hero, you immediately go up in your audience's esteem. This is true not just when the someone else is Elon Musk or Nelson Mandela, but also when they are another employee or a customer.

FORM

The form test checks that your story works when spoken aloud. The storytelling we are exploring is an oral art form. Speaking 'sounds' very different from the written word. Where writing tends to be more formal, speaking leans towards the natural and conversational.

When drafting your story, I urged you to keep it conversational. This is another important checkpoint. The only way to test if your story has 'oral form' (that is, it sounds like one person speaking to another) is to read it aloud. There is no other test as simple and effective.

Reading the story out loud, rather than in your head, hearing it as your audience will, is the only way to check for form at this point. But instead of just reading it verbatim, pretend you are *telling* it. Learn to tell your story out loud without looking at your notes. No peeping! It might be a leap of faith, but trust yourself. You already know the story well, because you drafted it.

Swot or not?

A golden rule for story mastery is never to learn your story off by heart, word for word. Swotting kills your story, making it sound mechanical. Do enough preparation to create a well-structured story that lands on message but that you can deliver it in a conversational way that engages your audience. I recommend learning your beginning and ending, but leaving the middle more organic. This puts you in the story sweet spot, illustrated in the following model.

FIGURE 10.1 STORY SWEET SPOT MODEL

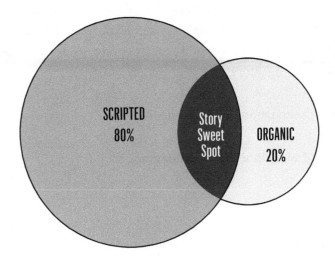

I introduced The Moth in chapter 8. Launched in 1997, The Moth's mission is to promote the art and craft of storytelling. The tagline for this global organisation is 'True Stories Told Live'. The Moth audience loathes anything overdone, over-scripted or over-performed. Moth events feature live storytelling.

At The Moth, as in business storytelling, the trick is to find the sweet spot between knowing what you will say and overcooking it. In fact, The Moth doesn't allow storytellers to have any notes on stage and recommends an unscripted approach in its guidelines.

I always advise my clients that stories are quite different from other communication forms. Stories work best when we don't nail down every word, work from a script or memorise it. In fact, these are three things that will doom your story to fail.

Substitution

To improve form, consider 'natural word substitution'. Always ask yourself, what would I normally say in this context? And use that. If you don't normally say words like esoteric and discourse, then don't put them in your story.

Would it sound more real if you said?

'Isn't Faust a little highbrow for grade 3?'

or

'Faust, in grade 3 – you are kidding me!'

Snakes on a Plane is a 2006 film that stars Samuel L. Jackson. It's so bad it became an instant cult film and meme. The title tells us the premise. A crime lord releases hundreds of deadly snakes on a commercial airplane to eliminate a witness, who is under Jackson's protection. Initial screening of the film (to test audiences) had no swearing in it. Yet swearing, and copious amounts of it, is likely the first thing anyone would do under the circumstances! So no swearing was unrealistic. The audience's vitriolic feedback made the producers edit the film and infuse it with expletives. So much so it is now very much a potty-mouth film.

I'm not advising you substitute profound with profanity in your stories. What I recommend is using substitution to keep it real.

Loading up

Another way to improve story form is to increase the sensory load of some words. Comics do this all the time. Compare 'he drank it quickly' with 'he swilled it down'. *Swilled it down* paints a picture. You immediately increase the sensory load for your audience. In storytelling, this is a good thing!

These two pieces of advice sound contradictory, but they actually help to balance your story. Using natural word substitution makes the story more human, conversational. Increasing the sensory load of one or two words enriches the story for your audience.

FINESSE

Finesse is about tweaking your story to give it panache! So often we find that somewhere in the process the story has become boring. Strip out the fun and load up with gravitas seems to be the aim. Not for a moment am I suggesting your story isn't important – it absolutely is. But robbing it of any lightness will work against you.

Finesse also means adding your own individuality to the story. It lets you do you, making it unique, like your fingerprints.

When Jackson Pollock worked on his large canvases he would use his whole body to spread the paint from all directions. He challenged the Western art tradition of using easel and brush. Using the technique critics came to call 'action painting', the artist expressed his individuality through his art. I urge you to find and unleash your inner Pollock! Or at least a humbler version.

The individual touches and flair in your story are your secret sauce as a storyteller. Here's an example.

STORY TITLE: ASKING THE RIGHT QUESTION

Peter Sellers! I love Peter Sellers. Just yesterday I was watching a YouTube clip from one of the *Pink Panther* movies where he plays Inspector Clouseau. Finding a large dog sprawled across the hallway, he asks the hotelkeeper, 'Does your durg bite?' That's my Indian version of Sellers' terrible French accent.

The man replies, 'No'. Peter Sellers reaches down to pat the dog and, wham, the dog attacks him! Peter Sellers turns to the man and says, 'I thought you said your durg does not bite'. The man replies, '*That* is NOT my dog'.

So much of our success in life depends on asking the right question.

STORYTELLER: YAMINI NAIDU

Anyone can watch this clip and share this story. Fans of Peter Sellers especially will enjoy it. I bring in my own identity (my poor imitation of Sellers' French accent), then joke about it. Just one line like that can turbo-charge your story, providing an opportunity for both humour and individual style.

For finessing, go to your strengths as a storyteller. Are you naturally funny? Do you have an unusual way with words, or do you use your whole body when sharing a story? Try to bring in these unique individual elements. Once you have done so, there is one final step in the finesse process.

Edit with a knife

Go back over the whole story. Be ruthless. Stand back and edit it with the knife of economy. Take stuff out, don't add stuff in. I am reminded of fiction writer Lelia Green's advice: 'Revising a short story is like being on an episode of *Hoarders*: you are surrounded by things you like and would love to keep, but should probably let go of for everyone's sake.'

Are there any unnecessary words? Does it have a saggy middle? Can you refine the ending further? You need to distance yourself from your story at this point. Ask of every phrase and every word, 'How does this serve the story?' Perform story triage, keeping whatever serves the audience and ruthlessly stripping out anything that doesn't.

Be careful about being overenthusiastic at this stage. You might end up with the shadow of a story or an anorexic story. Aim for the sweet spot between having an overblown story and one so brief it's over before it has even begun.

Title

Finally, give it a title. You won't use the title when sharing your story. It's just as a memory jogger for you. I'll often key it into my pitches, presentations or articles – 'Use Brussels sprouts here' or 'Share 2 apples'. (No, my weekly grocery list hasn't got mixed up with my business papers; these are titles of stories I plan to share.)

This is a wonderful discipline and helps you build your library of stories. It's also great fun – or that might just be the story geek in me.

Finessing your story gives your story its final edge.

In the next chapter we will look at how to nail delivery.

KEY INSIGHTS

- In pulling your beginning, middle and end together to craft a whole story, check for flow.
- Flow carries your audience through the story with you.
- You can make story outliers (stories that don't tap into existing schemas) work for you by giving your audience enough context.
- The form test checks that your story works when spoken aloud.
- Stories work best when we don't nail down every word, work from a script or memorise it.
- Word substitution (using words you normally use in conversation) and loading up with sensory detail increase story impact.
- Finally you finesse your story, adding your own individual touches, to give it panache.

11. DELIVERY – HOW TO GET LUCKY

Most of us associate delivery with the mechanics – stand here, look there, gesture this way. But delivery that focuses on the mechanics is like the little pigs that built houses of straw and sticks in the children's fable. The big bad wolf huffed and puffed and blew those houses down. The third pig was smarter and built a house of bricks that withstood the wolf's attack, and in the end the wolf met a gruesome death. Dark, I know. Is the wolf a metaphor for our fears? Read into it what you will. This chapter explores the secrets of delivery success that take storytelling beyond the pure mechanics. It's about building a house of bricks.

Delivery success starts way before you tell your story. Conference organisers once paid Jerry Seinfeld mega-dollars to present the secrets of his success. He duly mounted the stage stairs on the right and wrote three words on a whiteboard and exited stage left. Seinfeld had written 'DO THE WORK'!

I'M TOO SEXY FOR THE WORK

In the early nineties the British group Right Said Fred (the Fairbrass brothers) had a hit single called 'I'm too sexy'. If you haven't heard of it, I commend you on your good taste. If you have heard it, just remembering that title will have set off the ear worm in your head – sorry! The Fairbrass brothers ran a gym in London. In the gym there was lots of posing as people admired themselves in the gym's mirrors. While doing just that, as a joke one of the brothers took off his shirt and sang 'I'm too sexy for my shirt'. The song was born from this idea.

While some of us might be too sexy for our shirts, we are never too sexy for the work. Our delivery success starts right there. In this phase, we spend a lot of time getting clear on our purpose, carefully considering our audience and working on our beginning, middle and ending, before pulling it all together and paring it back to its essentials. Which is pretty much what I devoted the previous chapters of this book to. This work gives us the confidence we need for delivery. Avoiding any of this work, relying instead on just 'winging it', is a sure-fire way to fail.

When we write up our story (keeping it conversational), it pays to think in terms of drafting and redrafting the story to get it right. English fantasy author Terry Pratchett said, 'The first draft is you just telling yourself the story.' You then have to improve, refine and redraft it.

People ask, how should I share my story, where should I stand? The place to start is the solid base of the work you've already done. Now you hold in your hand a piece of story gold, or at least very polished coal, you can move into delivery mode.

Once you have your draft, you practise. This comes as a real surprise to many, including some of my clients. Yet it is practise that separates the winners from the rest. The golf champion Gary Player once said, 'The more I practise, the luckier I get.' There is no escaping the hard yards; it's practise, practise, and more practise.

There is a terrific line in the British-made TV drama *Killing Eve* (based on Luke Jennings' novel *Codename Villanelle*). Villanelle is a global assassin and public enemy number one. Witnessing her total badass behaviour a child asks, 'Is it hard to be bad?' And Villanella replies, 'Not if you practise'. Even being a badass requires practise!

LEVELS OF PRACTICE

I recommend two levels of storytelling practise. The first is aloud and alone.

You recite your story (not just in our head) and you listen to it. There is a huge difference between speaking your story out loud and running through it in your head. Speaking it makes it come alive, and you can sense where something is working or not.

But don't read it. Close your notepad or laptop and say it as you would to an audience.

'Do I have to learn my story off by heart, word for word?' This question polarises storytellers. To memorise or not. The truth is, memorising makes a story too mechanical, too perfect and scripted. It weakens the emotional connection you have with your audience. Think of a conversation. It's never word perfect. We falter, inject fillers like *um* or *er*, go back over things, search for the right words. This is the authentic, natural rhythm of conversation. We need this same spontaneity in our stories.

Yet we know we cannot leave this entirely to chance! So I suggest settling on a happy compromise. I'm all in favour of learning your beginning and your ending. Your beginning is where your nerves kick in, and starting with confidence helps you over this hurdle. It also helps you start strong, which is very important in grabbing your audience's attention. Memorising your ending also helps you land your story.

The middle of the story, though? Please keep that organic. You have done the work – now trust yourself. Stick to the structure without being a slave to it. That way you have the best of both worlds. A strong start, a fail-proof end – and an organic, spontaneous middle. This gives your story a conversational tone, which is very important for authenticity and connection.

Once you have practised your story aloud (walking the dog, in the shower or on the long drive to work are my three favourite practice settings), the next level of practise is to share your story with just one other person. Sharing it this way makes your story come alive. You tune into their body language and verbal feedback, then adjust accordingly. It is awkward with only one other person, but I say, 'Suck it up, princess!'

All my friends have learned to suspect my motives when sharing stories, say at a barbecue or at the pub. They always check if this is something that happened that I just want to share or if I am road testing a story for work. I plead the fifth!

Everyone has his or her favourite way of practising. Mine is to record myself into my phone and hear it back, or do it in the car. You may be afraid of sounding too rehearsed if you practise. Believe me, you won't. It's your material – you own it. I'd rather risk sounding too polished than coming across as unprepared.

ARE WE THERE YET?

Through drafting and redrafting, you now have a good version of your story. You have practised alone, and aloud and with someone else. Sometimes your trusted adviser may tell you the story is not there yet. GULP.

Don't panic, help is at hand. There are three reasons a story doesn't work:

- *Insufficient context.* You didn't provide your audience with enough context, so they couldn't follow your story. Dilruk Jayasinha, a Sri Lankan–born Australian comedian, does a whole comedy set on being asked for a durry. He was 19 years old, had just immigrated from Sri Lanka and had no idea what a durry was (learning only later it was a colloquialism for cigarette). As an immigrant, he was missing the context piece. If your story is about day-to-day stuff, like school or having a standoff with your boss, most people will already have a context in their heads and can easily join the dots. But it may be a problem if your story is about something arcane like beet farming or abstract expressionism or the *Cassini* space probe. Do you need to tweak your story to provide more context, without overwhelming your audience?
- *Something's missing.* Sometimes you may have used a conventional context yet the story still misses its mark. Check again to see if you missed out an important detail. Sometimes this detail (and it may be quite minor) is the pivot on which the story turns. Miss it out and your audience is lost, yet you are so close!
- *Oversold.* Sometimes we do the opposite by wringing everything out of a story. We spell it out and oversell it. This is tedious for our audience, who have already got the idea.

I endured a story by a consultant about how she dropped off her car for a check and the poor service she got. She drew it out, taking us through the interminable exchange, the car's problems, the complaint she lodged. It was predictable and boring – and fell totally flat.

I get there's a tension between these three reasons for failure. We might be so scared of overselling the story that we miss important details and therefore don't provide sufficient context. We could swamp our story with so much context and minutiae that we end up overselling it.

The following guidelines will help us through these murky waters.

When you practise your story before a test audience, pick someone unfamiliar with your work or context. That way you can test whether you have provided enough context. If the story works, then it is likely that you have included the important details.

Keeping your story under two minutes ensures you don't oversell it. Often we do our best work under such constraints. This time constraint forces you to strip your story down, which will prevent overselling. Combined with practising with a real person, this ensures you have provided enough context and haven't missed out a crucial detail.

Check out this story gem that ticks all these boxes, and still packs a punch!

STORY TITLE: SLOW DOWN TO SPEED UP

[CONTEXT] Yesterday I was talking to my team about our people engagement survey results. [IMPORTANT DETAIL] About how as a leader I can better support them to be their best at work, and whether they felt they had the tools to do their job.

To my surprise, one of them said, 'Every time we hear that a new project is expected to be delivered by yesterday, it makes us feel like we've failed, like we're behind before we've even had the opportunity to start'.

I realised then that as a leader sometimes you have to slow down to speed up.

STORYTELLER: CANDICE LIEW, AIA VITALITY

BUT WAIT, THERE'S MORE

And you thought this would be a simple stand here, look there, raise your right hand kind of chapter. So wrong! Let's look at some more elements that make your delivery rock.

Conviction

When you're sharing a story, the most important thing to communicate is your conviction. Do you see your story as a bit of a bore but something you have to share, or do you want to give it your best shot? Your conviction needs to be rock solid.

I am reminded of a scene in the British TV series *Absolutely Fabulous* (1992–2004), created by Jennifer Saunders and Dawn French. *Ab Fab* featured drug-addled public relations consultant Edina 'Eddy' Monsoon (Saunders) and her best friend, Patsy Stone (Joanna Lumley). This exchange was between the two of them and Edina's daughter Saffron.

SAFFY: Where are you going?

EDINA: New York.

SAFFY: I didn't think they let people with drug convictions in.

EDINA: Darling, it's not a conviction.

PATSY: Just a firm belief!

In storytelling, firm belief helps, but conviction propels you into success.

On Channel 9's reality TV show *The Voice*, Seal gave each of his team members a folded sheet of paper to prepare them for the battle ahead. Opening it, they read, 'There is nothing else there'. Imagine approaching your next story with this mindset, being 100 per cent present in your story. Your audience picks up on your conviction and mirrors this attention back to you.

Voice and poise

The most powerful thing you can do in your delivery is to imagine you're talking to only one person. Use a natural, everyday conversational tone. This might seem counterintuitive. Sadly, some people perform or act out a story in a story voice, which is guaranteed to make your story seem stagey, a setup instead of an authentic communication.

Poise is your conviction around the story. The audience can immediately sense this through your body language and pacing. No one will invest more in the story than you. Your engagement in the story cues your audience. If they sense it's important to you, they will also treat it as important.

Slow down, but not too much

One way I teach my clients to harness poise is to *slow down*. When you see fashion models on a runway, they stroll along, letting the clothes speak for themselves. There is flow and grace; not one of them is charging down the runway and hoofing back again! While that would amuse, no one would have time to absorb the clothes and the design aesthetic.

Most people who are new to storytelling rush through their stories. Usually it's nerves, because storytelling feels so different from every other form of communication they are used to. The audience leans in and listens, and the spotlight is squarely on them. Worry makes them hurry through, but this is a sure-fire way to bomb.

Go slow, but not so slow that it's annoying. You don't want to be like Kevin Malone (played by Brian Baumgartner) in the US television series *The Office*. Kevin is overweight and speaks really slowly, giving the impression he is mentally slow. In real life, the actor says people never hear his first sentences because they are so surprised that he is not a slow talker like his TV character!

One way to slow down with poise is to pause in key places in your story. Try counting to five in your head and see how this strategy works for you. When you slow down and savour your story, so will your audience. You are setting the bar, and the expectation that this will be worth it.

NO ONE IS GOING TO BE HURT

In *Writing Down the Bones*, author Natalie Goldberg's describes a *New Yorker* cartoon in which a man holding a rifle and a note-book addresses passengers on a plane: 'Now, sit still,' he says. 'No one is going to be hurt. I just want you to listen to a few of my poems.'

Goldberg is illustrating her point that poetry has never been massively popular, but this is not the case with stories. It might surprise you how avidly people listen when you share a well-crafted, purposeful, authentic story.

The texture of their attention is palpable. In a distracted, disrupted, fast-paced world this level of attention can feel like intense, wary scrutiny. It's not; it's the enchantment of an audience in rapture. Okay, maybe I got carried away there. More like an audience paying total attention.

At the end of your story, there's usually silence. Your audience will look at you without making a sound. For new and even seasoned storytellers this is unnerving. It can spook us. The silence is awkward. And just as nature abhors a vacuum, you'll want to fill that silence. Common mistakes are to explain the story, or make a weak joke (hello, anyone home?), both of which are heinous crimes, up there with explaining a joke or kicking a puppy.

Instead, revel in the silence. It's a golden space, because your audience is thinking about and feeling the power of your story. It's swirling through their mind, perhaps sparking memories or stories of their own. It's heading straight for their heart, bringing up positive emotions and attaching itself to their brain like velcro. Give your story the time and space it needs to make this journey. It's why I've found – and my clients affirm – that the results of storytelling are exponential (1+ 1 does not = 2; it's more like 200).

In business storytelling, silence is the equivalent of a standing ovation. Count to 15 in your head before moving on to whatever you want to say next. It requires nerves of steel, but like a karate master you build up to it, and you *can* do it.

REFLECT

After sharing your story, spend a few minutes reflecting on how it went. Ask someone in the audience you trust; read the Twitter feed; ask yourself what you should keep and what you would do differently next time. Reflection is a dish best served hot!

All of this sounds simple, but it takes discipline to do it every time, for every story. Way back in the first century, the Roman philosopher Seneca, who seems like a cool guy, nailed it when he said, 'Luck is where preparation meets opportunity'. See every story as an opportunity to shine, and prepare like mad to get there.

DELIVERY CONTEXTS

Understanding and harnessing the features of your context helps you deliver your story with maximum impact.

The three main contexts for storytelling are:

- one on one
- in a small group
- in a large group.

One on one could be in a hallway conversation or in a meeting or coaching session with a single employee or stakeholder. A small group could be a small team meeting with your peers or direct reports, or with other internal or external stakeholders. A large group could be your company town hall or some other large meeting or presentation. The Story Delivery Contexts Model helps us navigate these contexts successfully and for the biggest impact.

FIGURE 11.1: STORY DELIVERY CONTEXTS MODEL

	MINDSET	CONNECTION	INSPIRATION
BIG GROUP	Amplify	Scale	Powerful
SMALL GROUP	Authentic	Dispersed	Practiced
ONE ON ONE	Intimate	Tight	Prepared

Mindset

In the model, we look at the success mindset we need before we even embark on the delivery. The mindsets build on each other. One on one is obviously our most intimate setting. Our mindset is to embrace this intimacy. We are literally head to head, belly to belly, eye to eye with our audience.

We maintain this intimacy mindset even with a small group. Our attention may be more dispersed, but we always imagine we are talking to each individual personally. Don't let scale rob you of intimacy. You channel the same energy, whether you are speaking with one person or to a big group. But you amplify it when you need to.

Think of the first level in your one on one as building a fire to keep two people warm. To warm a larger group, you simply build up this fire. The size of the fire has changed, but it's still the same fire and it still keeps people warm.

In the two group contexts (small group and large group) we use stagecraft to scale our story.

Amplify with stagecraft

When I was a newbie speaker, moving on stage terrified me. I had an irrational fear of falling down or embarrassing myself. Then I worked with a brilliant coach and unlocked movement. Initially, it felt artificial, mechanical – move here and speak, then here. Then something clicks and you start to move naturally. Now I roam the stage like it's my personal savannah!

Don't let stagecraft intimidate you. It's just about using the space you have, such as moving across the stage as you speak.

Your body language must suit your context. In a one on one, or even a small group, sweeping gestures risk poking your audience in the eye! On stage, though, they can have a big impact. You don't have to use stagecraft, but in larger contexts like your company town halls, it can make your story pop. And for a story master it's essential.

Elements of basic stagecraft

On stage, any hand gestures have to be large. Hold your hands up from your waist and out to your sides. Arms fully outstretched at waist height indicates big; arms up in the air with fists closed says yes.

Your gestures have to match your words. Use a few gestures, but use them well. If you are saying three, then hold up three fingers. Nothing annoys your audience more than a disconnect between the visual and the spoken. Practise in front of a mirror.

Think of universal gestures. A shoulder shrug usually means I don't know. A hand to the head indicates thinking. We know this intuitively. In each instance, always go with the most natural gesture.

When moving on stage always move from right to left. In Western cultures, the right (your right when you're facing your audience) represents the past and your left shows the future. In your story timeline, you could begin on your right, move into the middle of the stage for the middle of your story and move left (and, for even more impact, forward) for the ending. Moving twice – for the middle of your story and for the ending – has a bigger impact than lots of random moves.

I recommend checking out Dr Louise Mahler's work on vocal intelligence and body language.

Connection

A story is a way of connecting with your audience. When you are one on one, the connection is tight. Often the 'audience' has no choice but to look you in the eyes. You want to maintain reasonable eye contact, though not with a first-to-blink-loses death stare.

In a small group, the connection is more dispersed, but it is important to make eye contact with everyone in the group. I like to do this in a random zigzag way so it's not predictable. And to ensure you aren't shooting furtive glances all around the room, spend two seconds longer just locking in on one or two people. Make sure you don't make them uncomfortable, though!

In a big group, the trick is to look at chunks of your audience at a time. You could look at the back left, then centre front, followed by the right middle.

The work you do with your eye contact keeps the connection between you, your story and your audience. This might sound simple but it's very powerful. So often, even at large conferences, you hear people say of a speaker, 'I felt she was talking just to me.' The simple strategy of making eye contact with your audience is one of the building blocks to amplifying intimacy through stagecraft. Think of a lighthouse, sweeping the horizon and guiding ships to safety. That is what you do with your eye contact, you are guiding the ship of your audience's attention through the story.

Inspiration

Ultimately, inspired storytelling is about always being prepared. You need to have done the hard yards around purpose, audience, story.

Practise your story a few times in different settings, especially one on one and in a small group. With each iteration your storytelling will get better. In comedy, you write your material but you build it through performance, which is where you find out what works, where the audience laughs, what to tweak. The same applies in storytelling. You write your story but build it through each telling. This is a new take on 'build it and they will come'! And it's how you have powerful storytelling in a large-scale context.

DELIVERY DO'S

The 1999 movie *The Hurricane* tells the true story of Rubin 'Hurricane' Carter, a talented American-Canadian boxer who was twice convicted of – and imprisoned for – the same murder. In the movie, his character says, 'He who bemoans the lack of opportunity forgets that small doors many times open up into large rooms'. The small things in storytelling can make a big impact. Nowhere is this truer than during delivery. While all these tips might sound small and obvious, together they pack a punch and set apart the story masters.

Conversational

Always remember that stories work best when they are conversational. We worked so had through the drafting and checking processes to keep the conversational tone, but it's especially important when delivering your story. The more conversational you keep this, the more impact your story will have. Look at seasoned come-dians: they always look like they came up with the content on the spot. Your story delivery should have this same feel to it.

Pros make it all seem so effortless. When they share a story, it is like they are sharing it for the first time, even though we know this is not true. So what's their secret?

Practise, but not too much

All pros practise, whether their field is sport, music ... or public speaking. No doubt Beethoven practised scales every day – possibly. Practise with real people and real content. But I find there comes a point when some of my perfectionist clients over-practise, sapping the energy of their story. I don't like to raise this too early, as some might see it as a get-out-of-jail-free card. This is not an excuse to abandon practise altogether. We've discussed this before. Practise, but don't nail down every word. It's about finding that sweet spot.

FIGURE 11.2: STORY IMPACT AND DIMINISHING RETURNS

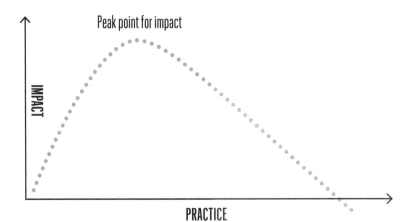

In this model, practise is measured by the x-axis and impact by the y-axis. With no practise, your story has little or no impact. With a reasonable amount of practise, your story achieves its peak impact. When you over-practise, it becomes mechanical, your impact drops off and the law of diminishing returns kicks in. Best to put that story aside and come back to it in a month or so, when you have forgotten every word.

Again, it's that sweet spot between being on script and structured (80 per cent) and being spontaneous (20 per cent).

Cueing an audience

Sometimes, without being unduly manipulative, we can cue an audience on what to expect, or even that the story has finished. In his inspiring memoir *Carry a Big Stick: A funny fearless life of friendship, laughter and MS*, Tim Ferguson shares his insight on how audiences like to be told what is expected of them: 'If you are after applause, trust me, the simplest signal is to throw your arms up in victory. It is a truth universally known that crowds want to act like crowds, even if there's no reason for them to do so.' And so much of their behaviour will mirror yours.

DELIVERY DONT'S

Here are three critical delivery don'ts to avoid at all costs.

Story voice

The first is using a story voice. This is an automatic sing-song voice people adopt when either reading out a speech or reading to children. The only way you'll be sure if you do this is to record yourself and listen back. Do you sound conversational or is there an up and down cadence? To your audience, a story voice sounds artificial, contrived, patronising. Practise your way out of that voice. The first stage is becoming aware if this is your default when telling a story. Sadly, no one will give you this feedback, so you have to self-test. If no story voice, hooray – you're doing well. If you detect a story voice, after that stiff scotch you need to put every effort into eliminating it completely. Yes, I insist on a zero-tolerance policy.

A piece of theatre

Business storytelling is about the everydayness. If you are with friends and sharing what happened to you when you missed the train to work, you don't suddenly jump up and start flinging your arms about dramatically, do you?

You might vary your voice and gestures and use humour. It's a mistake to treat your stories as theatre, because that puts your audience in spectator mode, *watching* you, when you want them to be in player mode, living this with you. In spectator mode something is being done to you – you are not part of the action. Spectator mode uses your pre-frontal cortex – your thinking, critical mode. So it also turns on your 'inspector mode'. You look at things as they unfold and inspect them to see what to improve or change. This is what overdramatising can do. Your audience enjoys it as a piece of theatre.

What you really want is for them to immerse themselves in your story – to feel it, to be it. And this happens best when you are more relaxed and everyday in your narration. You steer clear of excessive drama and acting out, which can be distracting even in a large-scale town hall context. The work you have already done is enough to immerse your audience. Any excessive theatricality feels like you are hamming, overdoing it. Restraint is your best friend here.

Stop improving

Don't ever stop improving. Hubris is your enemy. Keep thinking of different ways you could use your stories, elements you could tweak. Play with different beginnings and endings. A well-established speaker I know in Australia was presenting at a conference. Straight after him was an industry stalwart. My speaker friend, who lives the ethos of always improving, approached this industry star and requested feedback on what he could do better.

After watching him for the entire 60 minutes, the feedback came back: 'Wear something bright on stage – your tie, make it bright.' It was a 1 per cent offering, but my friend immediately adopted it. He also said he would never have thought of it on his own. So with every story, find the 1 per cent you can improve on.

MASTERY IN 15 MINUTES

How do you eat an elephant? asks an old riddle. One bite at a time. *How do you build story mastery?* You could spend 10,000 plus hours, as I have! Or you could do it five minutes at a time. Each time you share a story, going through the steps will help you to master that story. The three blocks of five minutes each are:

1. Practise.
2. Practise and perform.
3. Perform and reflect.

We master storytelling one story at a time and in five-minute blocks. A total of 15 minutes is needed to master one story, and it all starts with practise.

Practise

With a new story, spend your first five minutes as follows:

- Practise alone and aloud (2 minutes).
- Tweak the story (30 seconds).
- Practise with someone (2 minutes).
- Tweak the story (30 seconds).

Tweaking is making small modifications to improve your performance, like speeding up, pausing or changing words.

Practise and perform

Spend the second block of five minutes on practise and performance. This will help create a habit of always practising your stories before sharing them.

- Practise alone and aloud (2 minutes).
- Tweak the story (30 seconds).
- Perform/share the story (2 minutes).
- Tweak the story (30 seconds).

Practise, tweak (if needed) and then perform it by sharing it in a live context – for example, at a team meeting. Spend another 30 seconds tweaking it in your head if needed. What worked, and how might it be improved?

Perform and reflect

The third block is about performance and reflection. Each time you share the story, spend 30 seconds reflecting on how it went.

- Share story (2 minutes).
- Reflect on the story (30 seconds).
- Share story (2 minutes).
- Reflect (30 seconds).

What changes here is reflecting on the story – pausing to savour success, but also challenging yourself on what you could do better next time.

These story blocks and the steps through them sound simple, yet they hold the key to story mastery. It's all about consistency, doing this each time with every story.

The next chapter explores how you might move beyond mastery to story artistry.

KEY INSIGHTS

- Delivery success starts by doing the work, drafting and redrafting your story.
- There are two levels of practice – the first is aloud and alone, the second is with someone.
- The three story contexts are one on one, small group and large scale.
- Mindset, connection and inspiration help maximise your impact as a storyteller in each of these contexts..
- Keep your stories conversational, practise (but not too much), and learn to cue an audience.
- Don't use a 'story voice' or make your storytelling theatrical, and never stop improving.
- Master your stories, one story at a time, in five-minute blocks dedicated to practice, performance and reflection.

12. MASTERY TO ARTISTRY

What comes after mastery? Artistry. When I listen to Brené Brown, I am moved by her story artistry. The photographs of Diane Arbus (1923–71) are among the most widely recognised in the history of photography. Her images stand as powerful allegories of post-war America and are unforgettable to viewers. How did she scale such heights? She said, 'I am at war with the obvious.' And that is what artists do. In this section, we explore how we can become story artists. Some of these ideas may make you uncomfortable, but that is what artistry demands.

Attica is on the World's 50 Best Restaurants list, the cool guide to international dining. It is the only Australian restaurant to make the cut.

Ben Shewry, Attica's head chef and owner, says accolades don't drive him. What drives him are the standards he sets himself. In *Chef's Table*, a Netflix series that takes viewers behind the scenes, Shewry shares his journey. He talks about how he started by cooking Thai and European, then found his own voice. For him this meant going back to nature, using Australian produce and developing his own innovative dishes. An artist was born and Attica's success took root.

Research tells us that every child is an artist until age 9 or 10, when they see the gap between their drawing and the world around them. Sadly, this artistic crisis undermines their confidence in their drawing – many adults will tell you this is roughly when they stopped drawing.

Thanks in part to Seth Godin's ground-breaking work, we are no longer wedded to the narrow idea of an artist as someone who paints, draws or sculpts – who 'makes art' in a formal sense. Artists, rather, are people who excel in their field, so what they do seems almost magical.

If being a story master is not enough, then you might aspire to become a story artist, someone who can soar even higher in their storytelling practice.

AMATEUR TO ARTIST MODEL

This model outlines the journey from apprentice to artist. It maps a path to excellence and can be applied universally whenever we try to learn new things in life.

FIGURE 12.1: AMATEUR TO ARTIST MODEL

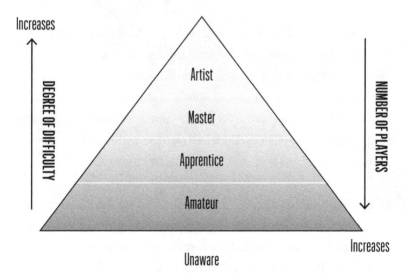

Some people are unaware they need to skill up. They don't know what they don't know. Any expert who has had conversations with someone ignorant of their field yet utterly confident in their views, which have somehow escaped being informed by experience, learning or evidence, will testify to this.

Some people think they can do this on their own. 'How hard can it be?' they say. It can work in some contexts and may be all we need for some jobs, but their efforts are generally amateur. Recently I couldn't sync my iCal and Google calendars on my phone. I was happy to embrace my amateur status and google the answer.

When people learn formally as newbies they find themselves in the apprentice phase of their learning. We don't have to climb this mountain in every facet of work and play. For example, instead of choosing to upskill, we can opt out or outsource. If there's something wrong with my car, I don't think to myself, what's the worst that could happen? and google the answer. Or count on upskilling and becoming an apprentice or master by watching YouTube videos. I outsource all my car issues to my trusted mechanic, who is a true master!

The difference between apprentice and master is about 10,000 hours, to use Malcolm Gladwell's oft-quoted metric. Sometimes the apprentice phase can serve us – we don't need a programmer's understanding of computer technology to use our laptop comfortably every day. But some people crave mastery. They want to excel. I guess that's you and that's why you picked up this book.

In the model, in any field, 40 per cent of the population is ignorant. Of the remaining 60 per cent, about 20 per cent will be amateurs (happy learning on their own from YouTube videos) and 20 per cent will progress to the apprentice stage. The numbers drop off as you near the top of the pyramid. About 15 per cent will crack the 10,000 hours, speeding up through knowledge and practice to achieve mastery. Then about 5 per cent, like Ben Shewry, break through this ceiling and become artists in their field.

Story artists are uniquely compelling storytellers. So what makes a story artist? The following advice will help you on your journey, which began long before we shared our first story.

Artists come in many shapes and forms, but no matter what their field they all share certain traits. They find and channel their unique talents. They are bold and original. Only when Ben Shewry found his unique 'voice' as a chef did his work and his restaurant come to national and international attention.

Let's look at some of the techniques that can help us on our artistry journey.

GET YOUR OFF-STAGE SH*T TOGETHER

Entrenched in our psyche is an image of the artist as someone who lives fast and dies young, who embraces a self-destructive hedonistic lifestyle that ends in a tragically early death. Think Amy Winehouse, Michael Hutchence and, well, sadly too many to name.

In case you're getting your hopes up, this is not a rallying call for this lifestyle. In fact, to be a successful story artist it is important first to get your off-stage sh*t together. Eat right, exercise, practise deep self-care – all this shows up when you show up. And it definitely shows up in your stories. You can't fake it.

It's hard to buy into a story about good life choices if the story-teller looks washed out, as if they haven't been making good choices, including getting to bed early the previous night. This might sound judgemental ... for gawd's sake it is, because your audience certainly will be. The first thing an audience looks for in an intuitive way is congruence. To persuade an audience, especially a smart, sophisticated audience, first we have to look like we have our own act together.

Even charlatans know this. The most shonky spruikers know to park a bright red Porsche outside the entrance to their seminar. It's such a cliché it should immediately get our guard up, but even that sham has been known to work in proving congruence. Our hopefully more sophisticated audiences aren't looking for flim-flam status symbols but a deeper congruence. And the artistry starts off stage.

THE X-FACTOR

I remember as a gormless twenty-something standing in front of my first Rothko at the Met in New York. I didn't understand what I was looking at, or even if it was the right way up, but it was so compelling I couldn't look away. It gave me goose bumps and brought tears. I found a Met volunteer guide, who explained the magic of Rothko. I was hooked!

I also credit this as the first time I realised that I too wanted to be a volunteer art guide. Many years later I achieved this ambition, and today I volunteer at the National Gallery of Victoria (NGV) in Melbourne. Even if you know little or nothing about art, you will probably recognise a Rothko or a Picasso. Because they are unique.

Perversely, much of our conditioning as children, at school, even through work and life, is towards conformity, weeding out individuality. Children, even rebellious teenagers, are keen to 'fit in'. The smooth functioning of our society depends on people following the rules. As humans, we feel a deep need to belong, to be part of the pack, and this too suppresses our individuality.

Artistry demands the polar opposite. It demands that we find our uniqueness, embrace it and celebrate it through our work and our stories. I have shared how I popped as a speaker only when I embraced my own identity. Today I am one of only a handful of Australian-Indian women speakers, in Australia and globally. This uniqueness is an advantage – it makes me stand out.

Where do you find your uniqueness? One place to start is to think about your strengths, what you do well, what you love doing. In my workshops, after participants share their story we give each storyteller a love bomb. We tell them what we loved about their story. I now ask the storytellers to write this down; otherwise, they might forget. Often what they write then is the start of their journey as artists. Because it's about what makes them or their story unique.

One of my clients got this love bomb: 'Your stories always make me laugh. Even in a serious story, you always have one line in it that cracks us up.' Until he received that love bomb, he did not understand that this was his X-factor. In the workshop he wrote it down. The next day he was so chuffed that he called me to discuss his love bomb. So often we dismiss our special talents: *Oh I'm sure everyone does that.* Please don't do this. The first step is to recognise this uniqueness, then you need to *own* it, because this is what will separate you (and your artistry) from the rest.

RISKY BUSINESS

So much of the vanilla in business comes from avoiding risk or anything that looks remotely unsafe. Taking no risks means our work is never memorable; it means we have settled for mediocrity. All artists know that with great risk comes great reward. Why is that?

Part of the human psyche is naturally resistant to change and novelty – 'the shock of the new', as Australian art critic Robert Hughes called it. Yet there is also a contradictory part of the mind that seeks the daring and exciting. The shock of the new is better than the shock of the boring!

Using a story that is startling as well as funny, personal and on point can be risky but offers a great reward: you shock your audience with the novelty, and your message sinks home. Predictability is a death knell in business, so strategic unpredictability makes you both an artist and a winner.

When we look back at the Amateur to Artist model, we see that at each stage the difficulty increases, but so does the risk. And the reward increases exponentially.

EXPERIMENT WITH THE EVERYDAY

From 1913, the artist Marcel Duchamp began placing ordinary objects – a bicycle wheel, a bottle rack, a urinal – in gallery installations. It shocked the establishment, who could not conceive of everyday objects (especially a urinal!) as art. With his embrace of the commonplace and ready-made, the artist made a radical art gesture. Like Duchamp, we look at everyday experiences and where others might see a urinal and a bicycle, with an artist's eye we see stories.

A certain cachet is attached to the title of *artist*, which conjures up ideas of exceptional, extraordinary, unique, one-off. But as story artists, our main material is the relatable everyday, which we present in new ways, just as Duchamp did.

Artists who experiment with the everyday don't rigidly follow the rules. In *How to Write about Contemporary Art*, Gilda Williams, suggests, 'I can't get no satisfaction may be grammatically incorrect but I can't get any satisfaction would murder the Rolling Stones song.' You can break rules to great effect, but breaking rules differs from being ignorant of the rules.

Artists look at the everyday and through observation, insight and risk transform it for their viewers, leaving the audience feeling, 'Wish I had thought of that!'

GOLD FOR YOUR VAULT

Leonard Cohen offered this advice to his nephew on wooing women: 'Listen well, then listen some more. And when you think you are done listening, listen some more.'

The same applies to story artists. To pan for gold, we have to be story listeners. To be a story artist requires that you see the world differently, but also that you're always listening for stories. Tune in daily to the frequency of *channel story*, which is *channel life*.

Artists are often ahead of the zeitgeist, or shape it. Every day I practise formal story listening. This is fun (though it sounds tedious). I scan my news feeds, my work with clients and daily stimuli for stories. Then I record the best of what I find in Evernote in a folder called 'A story a day'. It's a small daily ritual that feels like a 1 per cent, but in the exponential world of storytelling is so much more. Sharing this one practice with my clients has helped to transform them into story artists too.

Story listening is tuning in to life, what people are saying in and around work, that brief snatch of conversation you overhear when someone is chatting on their phone. Having a coffee and people watching, a walk in the park. All are story listening opportunities.

This ephemeral material must be captured before it is lost. I record clients' stories, but will always approach them for their written permission before using it. Some have completely forgotten that story, even though it was powerful and moved everyone in the room. This no longer surprises me, given the vagaries of human memory, but I strongly recommend that you don't leave your stories to chance. Recording them is like putting your gold in a vault: you know where it is and can access it whenever you need to.

BEGINNER'S MIND, ZEN MIND

'How do they get non-stick material to stick on non-stick pans?' A user question posed to Richard Cornish, the columnist of 'Vexing Culinary Questions' on the *Good Food* website. Puzzled and unable to answer, he asked his eight-year-old daughter. 'Simple,' she replied, 'It's non-stick on one side only!'

Ahh, the genius of kids. It's what Zen masters call 'the beginner's mind' – curious, no tunnel vision and open to possibilities. Sadly, it's a quality we lose when we leave childhood behind. As adults, fear of failing, particularly in public, can shut down our beginner's mind. The British philosopher, writer and television presenter Alain de Botton explains it like this: 'Why we fear failing is not just a loss of income, a loss of status. What we fear is the judgement and ridicule of others. And it exists.'

Kids, who think anything is possible, take risks – and sometimes succeed. Looking good in front of their peers doesn't cross their minds. Peter Stillman designed an activity titled the Marshmallow Challenge (which was later popularised by Tom Wujec in his TED talk 'Build a tower, build a team'). Teams of four were given the following resources:

- 20 strands of uncooked spaghetti
- 1 yard of string
- 1 yard of tape
- 1 marshmallow
- 18 minutes.

The goal was to build the tallest freestanding structure. Only one rule: the marshmallow must be on top. Stillman conducted marshmallow challenges all over the world with diverse teams, including engineers, business school students, leaders and entrepreneurs. His most astonishing finding: 'Kindergarteners on every objective measure had the highest average score of any group I have ever tested.' Kindergarteners consistently outperformed the adults. Or, as Stillman put it, 'kindergarteners kicked ass!'.

The beauty and joy of the beginner's mind. Think of what story challenge you can bring a beginner's mind to today.

STAY WORTHY

In *Everybody Lies*, author Seth Stephens-Davidowitz shares this anecdote: 'Amazon engineer Greg Linden introduced doppelgänger searches to predict readers' preferences, the results were so good that Jeff Bezos fell to his knees and shouted I am not worthy!'

Bezos knows to stay humble and to always be learning. In some sense true artists have the mind of a child, knowing there's always more to learn. The paradox is that artists produce their best work when they see themselves as apprentices. The fashion designer Givenchy famously designed Audrey Hepburn's elegant look – the sleeveless sheath dress with a row of pearls. Yet he called himself the 'eternal apprentice' constantly searching for new inspiration and ideas.

SELF-COMPASSION AND NON-ATTACHMENT

Storytelling is not like a maze where alarms go off if you make a mistake and burly guards escort you out. So always practise self-compassion with your stories. Don't beat yourself up over every mistake. The mistakes in your story keep it real. In conversation we are not word perfect, we go back over stuff; we take time to think. All this keeps the authentic magic in your storytelling.

There is a second part that helps us with our self-compassion. While we put in the blood, sweat and tears, we also remain non-attached to the outcome. Nothing deadens the impact of a story more than the teller overinvesting in its impact. Non-attachment/detachment sounds very Buddhist, but it can give your story the right energy. You did the work. You hope the story serves your audience. This gives you a quiet sense of conviction.

In *Writing Down the Bones,* Natalie Goldberg shares this profound example of non-attachment: 'In Japan, there are stories of great poets writing a superb haiku and then putting it in a bottle in a nearby river or stream and letting it go.'

PRACTISE HANAMI

In April this year I was in Tokyo working with Goldman Sachs on business storytelling. My trip coincided with the cherry blossom season. Nothing prepares you for the beauty and bliss of this unique sensory experience. Cherry blossom season is fleeting, the magic ephemeral, and after a short, intense period the beauty disappears all too soon.

The Japanese celebrate this season through the practice of hanami, which is the art of contemplating the transient beauty and fragility of flowers (especially cherry blossoms) when in full bloom. It could be a walk through the park or sitting on viewing benches in front of the trees or attending a picnic under the blooms. It is an act of both contemplation and celebration.

How can we bring hanami into our storytelling? How about taking time out to contemplate and reflect on our stories, instead of relentlessly surging forward to conquer the next story, the next item on our to-do list, the next project?

I believe we can and should apply hanami specifically to storytelling, but more broadly in our life and work. My interpretation of hanami is about making the space in our lives for pausing, contemplating and celebrating. Something as simple as three deep breaths can help. Sitting down in our favourite café and savouring that perfect cup of coffee, instead of rushing off with a takeaway cup. Walking through a park on the way to the office. Looking deeply at a work of art, immersing ourselves in its beauty. Stopping to listen to a busker.

Hanami can be imagined as a micro-holiday at work. It creates more time and energy for us to take our creative instincts deeper, to do our best work, to savour life's joys and to produce our best stories.

KEY INSIGHTS

- To become story artists, we have to move into our uniqueness, to be bold and original with our storytelling.
- Artistry starts with getting our off-stage sh*t together, then finding our x-factor and taking risks.
- Risks require us to experiment, not with outlandish ideas but with the every day.
- True artistry gold is in our story listening, and we have to mine this story gold and put it in our vault by recording the stories.
- Even though we pride ourselves as artists, our ongoing success depends on adopting a beginner's mind and staying humble.
- Practising hanami – making space in our lives for pausing, contemplating and celebrating – is something we should do not just in relation to storytelling, but in all our work.

LET'S CONNECT

Every writer has only one wish – to be read – and it's readers like you who make that wish come true. So thank you.

I invite you now to embrace the spirit of action, knowing that action brings rewards that hubris cannot.

Even in the midst of the most daunting, unimaginable change, remember the timeless words of Plato: 'The beginning is the most important part of the work.' So what is the smallest step you can take today towards becoming a story master?

I'd love to partner with you on this journey, so please connect with me on my website
yamininaidu.com.au
... or on LinkedIn
linkedin.com/in/yamininaidu

I wish you all possible courage and good fortune on your journey to Story Mastery.

Now stop reading and get to it!

Best wishes,

Yamini

APPENDIX

100 STORY IDEAS

I'll leave you with a gift of a 100 story ideas (and two bonus ideas). Some of these ideas nest thousands of stories, so it's truly a gift that keeps on giving. For example, the Moth website and podcast feature live storytelling events in cities around the world.

Follow the links. You'll still have to craft your story, using the tools I have shared in this book, but this resource will ensure your story wells never run dry!

1. Google doodle each doodle tells a story, https://www.thesun.co.uk/news/6501888/ euenie-brazier-google-doodle-french-chef-birthday/
2. TED talks
3. Moth podcasts (and here's a link to my Moth video: https:// youtu.be/Ds3H_sv-LwM)
4. Best holiday you ever had
5. Worst holiday you've ever had
6. Best Christmas
7. Worst Christmas
8. Travel tales
9. Proposing to your partner, or being proposed to
10. Falling in love for the first time
11. Learning to drive

12. Moving house
13. Joining a new school
14. Having your first child
15. Finding out you are going to be a parent
16. The best customer service experience you ever had
17. The worst customer service experience you ever had
18. Your favourite sporting moment
19. Your most gut-wrenching sporting moment
20. Hobbies
21. Your childhood
22. Your favourite teacher
23. The worst teacher you ever had
24. The school bully
25. Your first date
26. The worst date you ever had
27. Your pets
28. Travelling overseas for the first time
29. Your favourite meal
30. Your best dinner memory
31. That dinner disaster
32. How you met your best friend
33. How someone stood up for you (had your back)
34. The funniest thing that ever happened to you
35. The funniest thing that ever happened to someone you know
36. Odd spot from *The Age* newspaper, which features weird and wonderful stories from around the world, https://www.theage.com.au/national/odd-spot-20080306-ge6t7j.html
37. Newspaper cartoons
38. Favourite film
39. Favourite scene from a film

40. Favourite book
41. Favourite fictional character
42. Person you admire
43. Celebrity whose antics make you roll your eyes
44. Today's newspaper
45. Your family
46. A protest march you've been on
47. The best gift you ever received
48. The worst gift you ever received
49. Favourite business book
50. Words of wisdom from a mentor
51. Favourite memory about your grandparents
52. Scour business books for stories
53. *Bad Girls Throughout History: 100 Remarkable Women Who Changed the World* by Ann Shen contains 100 stories most people would not have heard about. One gem: the story of Khutulun, the Mongol warrior and athlete who wrestled men and won all their horses.
54. Your favourite book as a kid
55. Your worst travel tale
56. buzzfeed.com
57. *Time* magazine's annual feature on the world's most influential people
58. Nobel prize winners in different fields. Research their stories.
59. *Time* magazine's 100 most iconic photos
60. *New Scientist's* 21 great mysteries of the universe
61. Fast Company's list of world's 100 most creative people
62. Favourite TV show when you were growing up
63. What specific memory/experience/place makes you nostalgic?
64. Describe a time in your life when you faced uncertainty and what happened.

65. Describe a challenge you faced and the lessons you learned from it.
66. Describe an 'aha' moment in your life and whether it still influences your behaviour.
67. Describe a time you persisted in order to achieve something.
68. Share one of your regrets and why you regret it.
69. Describe a turning point in your life, and why it had such an impact.
70. Share a time you pursued a dream.
71. Describe a situation in which you faced conflict and how it challenged you.
72. Describe a time you believed in yourself and achieved something against the odds.
73. Podcasts are packed with stories (every time you hear one, make a note).
74. Share an example of when you saw a small change at work make a difference for stakeholders.
75. Describe a time when your workplace simplified a process or system with great results.
76. Describe a time when you felt proud to work in your organisation.
77. Describe a time when you or someone you know received positive feedback from a stakeholder.
78. Give us an example of something you have seen or heard recently at work that inspired you.
79. Share a time when you went home excited about something that happened at work.
80. Share a time when you offered a simple solution that made a difference for your customers/stakeholders.
81. Describe a time when you or someone you know at work did the right thing for a customer.

82. Have you heard a customer describe a positive experience they have had with you or a team member?

83. Describe a time when you or someone you know delivered a great customer experience.

84. Share a time when you or someone you know had positive feedback from a customer, colleague or supplier.

85. Describe a time when someone at work shared a positive experience with your organisation.

86. Share a time when your company did the right thing (for you, a colleague, a supplier or the community).

87. CEO Guru, BBC, https://www.bbc.com/news/business-20071226

88. ABC RN presents arts, books and culture in The Hub, http://www.abc.net.au/radionational/programs/the-hub/

89. 19 of the most inspiring rags-to-riches stories in business, *Business Insider*, https://www.businessinsider.com.au/best-rags-to-riches-stories-2015-10?r=US&IR=T

90. 5 World Famous Business Success Stories, https://successstory.com/inspiration/5-world-famous-business-success-stories

91. 8 Great Entrepreneurial Success Stories, https://www.entrepreneur.com/article/243099

92. Google searches on failure stories

93. Reddit gives you the best of the internet in one place. Get a constantly updating feed of breaking news, fun stories, pics, memes and videos just for you, Reddit.com

94. *Wired* magazine, wired.com

95. Fast Company is the world's leading progressive business media brand, with a unique editorial focus on innovation in technology, leadership and design. Check out the sections on ideas, leadership, technology, www.fastcompany.com

96. Check out Plot Generator, https://www.plot-generator.org.uk/ (more for fiction but gets your story idea justices flowing)

97. Check out review sites like Yelp and Trip Advisor (packed with stories)
98. Google search for these terms
    - inspirational business success stories
    - business success stories from rags to riches
    - successful business people and their stories
    - successful entrepreneurs and their stories
    - success stories of entrepreneurs in India
    - business success stories
    - successful entrepreneurs stories.
99. Obituaries
100. NPR StoryCorps, an independent non-profit project with the mission to honour and celebrate the lives of everyday Americans by listening to their stories, https://www.npr.org/podcasts/510200/storycorps

INDEX

Story examples

CPSIA information can be obtained
at www.ICGtesting.com
Printed in the USA
FSHW021346011119
63650FS